BENDABLE LEARNINGS

The WISDOM
of MODERN MANAGEMENT

Also by Don Watson

Caledonia Australis
Recollections of a Bleeding Heart
Death Sentence
Watson's Dictionary of Weasel Words
American Journeys

BENDABLE LEARNINGS

The WISDOM *of* MODERN MANAGEMENT

DON WATSON

with Helen Smith

KNOPF

A Knopf book
Published by Random House Australia Pty Ltd
Level 3, 100 Pacific Highway, North Sydney NSW 2060
www.randomhouse.com.au

First published by Knopf in 2009

Addresses for companies within the Random House Group can be found at
www.randomhouse.com.au/offices.

National Library of Australia
Cataloguing-in-Publication Entry

Watson, Don, 1949–
Bendable learnings: the wisdom of modern management / Don Watson.

ISBN: 978 1 74166 904 6 (hbk)

Sociolinguistics.
English language – Terms and phrases.
Jargon (Terminology) – Social aspects.
Management – Terminology.
Business – Slang.

306.44

Cover illustration by Alberto Ruggieri/Illustration Works/Corbis
Internal illustrations by Bruce Petty
Cover and internal design by Natalie Winter
Typeset in Bembo by Midland Typesetters, Australia
Printed and bound by Griffin Press, South Australia

Random House Australia uses papers that are natural, renewable and recyclable
products and made from wood grown in sustainable forests. The logging and
manufacturing processes are expected to conform to the environmental regulations
of the country of origin.

10 9 8 7 6 5 4 3 2 1

For John Timlin

Contents

In due time the fraud is manifest, and words lose all power to stimulate the understanding or the affections.

Ralph Waldo Emerson, *Nature*, 1841

The strategy is the strategy and the returns are the returns.

Bernie Madoff, 2007

Introduction

In my youth the local town had three fish and chip shops. One of them served chips that were dun-coloured and thick, crisp on the outside with white, floury and fearfully hot insides. At another they were wan and waxy, long and bendy, on the slimy side and always a little undercooked. At the third shop, Vic's Chippery, the hirsute and mountainous Vic Moskos sliced his potatoes very thin. Vic was an iconoclast: while fish and chips everywhere came wrapped in newspaper, Vic put his in a wax-paper bag where the chips sweated and stewed with the fish and batter. Vic's Chippery supplied the high school, and I have few more stimulating memories of my secondary education than feeling about with my fingers in the sweltering interior of those bags and conveying to my mouth pieces of the congealed, vinegary pulp.

Now, consider a bucket of McDonald's chips – or 'fries', as they have become. Consider them, as Michael Pollan does in *The Botany of Desire,* as the Platonic ideal of French fries: 'slender golden rectangles long enough to overshoot their trim red containers like a bouquet'.[1] The potato abstracted, globally: so abstracted, it is likely that many people who eat McDonald's fries are unaware or have forgotten that it is potato

---

1 Michael Pollan, *The Botany of Desire*, Bloomsbury, London, 2002, page 244.

that they're eating. Just as likely, if they do think of the fries as potatoes, the only breed of potato they have ever tasted is the kind McDonald's demands of its growers and sells not so much as potato as a brand made from potato. That kind is the unnaturally elongated, uniform and almost eyeless Russet Burbank, or in very recent times an even more sophisticated Monsanto invention, the New Leaf.

The subtle differences of flavour, fragrance and texture which distinguish one kind of potato from the many others that exist are unknown to most of the world's regular potato-eaters. Floury and waxy, big, small, smooth and gnarled, deep eyes and shallow ones, sweet, aromatic and bland potatoes, potatoes that bake well and potatoes best mashed, potatoes with red soil or black or grey soil still sticking to them. Green potatoes, new potatoes – when did you last see new potatoes? I mean potatoes both for eating and for talking about: subjective, nuanced, paradoxical, real potatoes; not just carbohydrates but the rudiments of life.

Now consider this, from the current Premier of Victoria. It is a sentence very like many other sentences the Premier utters when he speaks to the public and the media. This is his way of telling us what our government is doing and intends to do and why. It is the way most premiers keep their electors informed.

> *What we do have in this state, I think, is an exciting agenda,*
> *going forward, a very positive agenda in terms of education*
> *and health, and we've also got some big challenges there that*
> *we, you know, need to get on top of.*[2]

Imagine this sentence broken at random into bits and arranged in the McDonald's bucket like fries. It's a bit wordy, so we can take out everything up to *exciting agenda* and everything after

2 Premier of Victoria, press conference, 25 February 2008.

challenges – unless you are especially keen to get on top of them. This will leave room for his next sentence that day: *'And I've indicated that public transport is an issue in our state'* – which was to say, he had 'indicated' that something the public knows from maddening experience was an 'issue', though not to say why he thought we needed to know that he had 'indicated' what we already knew, or why countless cancelled train services were an 'issue', as opposed to a pain in the neck or a consequence of bad management or policy. Try not to think about it; just put it in the bucket and move on to the next sentence:

> *I've announced a number of initiatives in terms of improving our public transport system, but tackling congestion in public transport and on the roads remains a key agenda issue for me, going forward.*

That should be enough for the bucket, though it's a pity to leave out the *number of exciting initiatives to address some of the issues*, which appeared in the sentence following, and the *commitment* in a later one, and finally: '. . . *at the end of the day, the market is the test in these things and, you know, the market has not supported it in a way which is viable, going forward.'* We could probably squeeze all of that in, and if we can't, we can leave out a couple of spare *initiatives* and *issues*. What you have, then, is a bucket that looks like this:

As McDonald's customers find in the bucket everything they need in the way of potatoes, modern managers (a category that includes modern premiers) will find in this bucket everything they need to make sentences. This is the meat and potatoes of politics and management – without the meat. And there's no nourishment in the potatoes. And, although it is almost certain they are *committed to diversity*, no variety. In truth, the Premier might have assembled his words in all manner of other combinations and still said much the same thing – that is to say, nothing of consequence.

Among politicians, making the obvious or trite sound profound is an ancient habit. A federal minister on the banks of the Hume Dam tells us that:

> *[the] two years prior to the election of this government*
> *were the driest two years in terms of the Murray River in*
> *history . . . So this is an historically dry circumstance we all*
> *find ourselves in.*[3]

What leads a minister to call a drought 'an historically dry circumstance' is a mystery that perhaps even she cannot explain, but its roots might be in the same soil as her prime minister's observation, at the same place on the same day, that 'to deal with the long-term challenge of climate change, we need to act and we need to act with a clear-cut course of action.'

We are not saying the prime minister and his colleagues are idiots. Judge them by their professional success, by most that they do, and they come up more than tolerably smart and well informed. We see no signs of simple-mindedness except on some occasions when they speak. Then we suffocate in their platitudes and their brainless managerial locutions. This sheer

---

3 Prime Minister of Australia, joint press conference with the Minister for Climate Change and Water, 14 July 2008. The Minister was reported saying *'driest in terms of'* but the PMO press release has her saying *'direst in terms of'*.

vacancy of expression is not constant. They can do better. But it happens too often to be called *a non-ongoing event*. The challenge calls for them to *act with a course of action*. The issue calls for *initiatives going forwards*. The years were the driest *in terms of the Murray River* – as if the years have a relationship with the river that can be measured in the same way that mathematics measures one precise thing *in terms of* another.

That scrofulous cliché *in terms of* is an unfailing symptom of the pseudo-science at the bottom of managerial language. Managerial language is today's public language, the language of politicians, bureaucrats and chief executives; of all managers, in other words, including the captains of cricket teams who, with no apparent strain, are likely to tell us that Andrew Symonds might 'impact the team in his personality' or that Herschelle Gibbs has 'made an effort in terms of improving his lifestyle'.

To save my life, I could not speak credibly about economics for ten seconds, yet I can see why the financial bubble took so long to burst. It was because all that financial *innovation* was manifestly good. So good and so manifest that, whether it was in making millions or having a title to their own modest home, it inspired wonder in those who felt the benefits: wonder at the great and mysterious power of the market that *innovation* unlocked for them; wonder at the genius of the market, and at the power the market moved in them. A New York hedge fund manager told me in 2005 that he could not account for his dizzying success without believing in 'some . . . greater force' – he did not have a word for it. An earlier generation would not have hesitated to call it Providence. We are less articulate about the nature of the divine, and more likely to claim all the credit for ourselves, but people like that hedge fund manager are co-religionists with the old capitalists in the sense that they are believers; and believers are believers, whether they believe in God's tremendous ear or the robustness of the distributional assumption.

It is much harder for an economics ignoramus to explain why the bubble burst: to what degree cleverness, cupidity, Alan Greenspan or faith in the efficient-markets hypothesis brought about systemic failure. As ever, such questions can only be answered by experts. Let the ignorant choose their favourite. What seems a safe conclusion is that the world financial system was built on all kinds of bogusness – the more bogus, the more pretending to predictive science. The dogma of free markets, the new credit *instruments*, the disguised conflicts of interest among the credit-ratings agencies, the compliance of governments and central banks – it was all phoney. And the language with which insiders persuaded themselves and each other that their schemes were downright inspired, and the rest of us that they were at least sound – the language was phoney too. This perverse, cabalistic, technocratic language was part of the general folly.

In the year that I met the hedge fund manager, another wealthy American investor explained to me why the financial crash was coming. It had to come, he said, and it would be worse than any crash since 1929. In 2005 I had not heard of the sub-prime market, of derivatives or credit swaps or any of the other new financial products he described, and I could not understand a tenth of what he said. Bereft of technical understanding as I was, he could have talked all day about the 'lagged value of the term spread' and illustrated it with a dozen PowerPoint slides and still I would have gone home unmoved and oblivious to the danger.

But some things must have touched the nerve ends of my inner Jeremiah. When he gave me something concrete – such as that thirty-five per cent of loans in the previous year were unsecured; that these new *products* had exposed the world's biggest financial institutions to dodgy, massively overvalued assets and debt that could not be repaid; that paying financial industry executives millions in bonuses had encouraged them to take greater and greater risks – in a trice, the Babylonian army was racketing at the gates.

No doubt, in what remains of the financial industry, people are still using the buzzwords and pretending to science, but not so often in places where the rest of us can hear it. At last we hear words we recognise, even if it takes an effort of memory: words like *greed*, *corruption* and *stupidity*, which describe concrete things with more precision than the technical language they have replaced. What other words will do for the $6 billion in bonuses paid to Merrill Lynch executives in 2006, or the $46 million that company's chief executive was paid that year, in a country that cannot come up with a decent health system and where 50 million workers are paid less than $10 an hour? *Corruption* and *greed* are apt words for it. And when you read how an alleged $7.6-billion profit one year became insolvency and a taxpayer bailout the next, *stupidity* is pretty well the first word that comes to mind – though *innovation* is another possibility.

Innovation has much to answer for. George W. Bush always said it was to 'encourage innovation' – and its cousin, 'entrepreneurship' – that he gave those tax cuts to the rich in 2001. The cuts encouraged a colossal deficit and outrageous inequality instead. Those grotesque executive salaries were justified as 'incentives to innovation'. 'Pay for performance' rewarded strenuous effort (or 'efforting') and bright ideas among everyone from CEOs to real-estate appraisers; it also encouraged them to take silly risks, hide losses and 'loot the place through seemingly normal corporate mechanisms'.[4] It was in the name of innovation that the masters of the financial universe came up with *securitised loans* – that is to say, loans packaged and onsold in ways that made them less secure. Innovation gave us all kinds of *leveraging*, which is what you

---

4 Bill Black, quoted by Thomas Frank in *The Wall Street Journal*, 4 February 2009.

do with assets when, if you didn't, you'd be in debt. From innovation came *liar loans*, and *credit default swaps* and *derivatives*: instruments that Warren Buffett called 'financial weapons of mass destruction'. Another whiz said they 'need to be banned because nobody understands them and few are rational enough to know it'.[5]

'Financial innovation', the Board of the US Federal Reserve declared in 2004, has 'rendered nearly irrelevant' the regulations imposed on financial markets by the Depression-era Bear-Steagall Act. In 1999, after much expensive lobbying the act was repealed by congress, and investment banks and commercial banks were no longer kept apart and out of temptation's way. Of course, the repeal of the act had nothing to do with corruption, greed, lies or stupidity. When you spend $300 million lobbying congressmen, you get to choose your own words – so it was called the 'Financial Services *Modernization* Act'. Since it created pre-1930 conditions for 'financial services', it might just as well have been called the 'Financial Services Deregulation Act'. Or the 'Regression Act'. Or the 'Self-Interest Act'.

When we talk of *embedding innovation* in legislation, or in company *cultures*, or in departments of housing or finance, or in local councils or schools, we *embed* a platitude – a husk of a word with just the pretence of truth, little different from a fiction or a lie. Of course, an organisation is often better for being innovative. It is not a bad ambition to have – to introduce something new. So long as the new is better than the old. But the word itself does nothing very useful: most often it is nothing more than a box to be ticked, a little god to which obeisance must be rendered, as if by intoning 'innovation', managers – and politicians – might call up all the secret powers of capitalism and its high priests (Adam Smith's invisible hand, Joseph Schumpeter's creative destruction, Ayn Rand's rational

5 Nassim Nicholas Taleb, *Financial Times*, 7 April 2009.

self-interest), and thus bring good fortune on their enterprise.

Yet, at the same time as they swear by innovation, modern managers demand the most rigid adherence to company values and goals, and they impose on the world a language in which it is all but impossible to express clear and original thoughts – in which it's difficult even to have clear thoughts, or any thoughts. Utter it as often as you like, the word won't help you think anew; and even if it did, your thoughts might not be good ones or better than your old thoughts. More likely, in an *innovative culture* inferior thoughts – including flawed or stupid thoughts – might be preferred over good ones for no better reason than the newness with which they satisfy the creed of innovation.

No one dies, of course. Or to put that another way: 'Whatever the adverse outcomes, in terms of language, death is not one of them, very often.' It is not *key*. The present financial crisis will pass. It will wreak its creative havoc and leave us with a new, well-regulated economic order, on which the world's next generations may depend. At least let us imagine such a happy future. But in this new order what language will our leaders and managers speak? What will be the language of work and education? Will the new economic order discard all those abstract nouns that require equal numbers of *in terms of* to hold them together, and hardly fewer *impacts* for when they meet? Will they still call education *learnings*? Will they still describe sacking staff as a *synergy-related headcount reduction*?

Management's language has evolved to fill management's needs. It came in on the back of management theories which, though numerous and various, are all concerned with 'the art of getting things done through people'. Innovation, marketing, logistics, profits – all these are material questions for management, but they all depend on the matter of people. Modern management theory has decided that to get the most out of people, an organisation must command loyalty to certain *values* and *aims*, participation in a common *culture* and employees who are all but reflexive in dealing with demands of their work. Management theory is an ideology and, like other ideologies, it uses language to consolidate power and to direct and modify behaviour.

We know that such is the complexity of the human brain and its relationship with experience that 'each individual perceives the world in a unique way'.[6] It is the principle task of the manager – or the mullah or the commissar – to limit the expression and consequences of this characteristic of the human condition. In their corporate governance, their mission and vision statements, it is all but mandatory for organisations to declare their belief in *diversity* and their faith in the talents of *their people*. Yet in almost every case the reverse is true: indeed, all their organising principles, including the central one of language, lead towards an ever more rigorous monoculture, which, if translated to politics, might be mistaken for a squadron of Red Guard or Jehovah's Witnesses.

If management were truly interested in the potential of diversity they would surely prefer the model of, say, the Rockefeller Institute, arguably the most successful organisation of the last century. Though built upon a principle of diversity, the Rockefellers' phenomenal contribution to scientific knowledge was made without resort to *team-building exercises*, *branding*, *buzzwords*, *goal alignments*, or any other *effortings* in pursuit of *buy-in* or *groupthink*. Of course, an oil company and a research institution are unlikely to be equally suited by the same organisational model; but then the same applies to an oil company and a department of education, or a merchant bank and a swimming team.

6 J. Rogers Hollingsworth, 'High Cognitive Complexity and the Making of Major Scientific Discoveries', in Arnaud Sales and Marcel Fournier, *Knowledge, Communication and Creativity*, Sage Publications, California, 2007, page 146.

In a sense, management language deserves our admiration; like many successful weeds, pests and viruses, it has adapted and thrived. Nuance, humour, irony, metaphor, invention, streams of consciousness or fancy, the vernacular – hundreds of elegant and useful words and phrases have gone the way of the telex and the roneo machine. Management language elbowed aside everything that a modern organisation did not need. It strangled original thought. What the market could not turn into commodities management could – with language. Everything, including a ten-year-old child's schoolwork, became *product*. The arts became an *industry*; artists, practitioners and works of art, *artworks*. Football players became *accountable* and played *accountable football*. Every drongo wanted *closure*. Whoever they were and whatever they did, managers addressed their charges in management buzzwords, and only when the answers came back in the same terms did they feel secure in their authority.

Whatever the shape of the new economic order, the language is sure to continue on its present depressing course. Can anyone imagine a premier sometime in the future speaking to us in a spontaneous and amusing way? One might as well imagine a government department that isn't *values-driven*, a bank that isn't *customer-focused*, schools that teach rather than *deliver learnings* and *outcomes*. Far from retreating, the public language will increasingly invade the private sphere: the patio, the spa, the gymnasium, the bedroom.

There will be refuseniks, of course, and not all of them in nursing homes. They will continue to speak and write in whole sentences, use concrete words and phrases, recite poems on their bicycles and 'fasten words again to visible things'. It will be a kind of boutique language, spoken by a substantial minority, perhaps with their own FM radio station and wearing small badges on their lapels. Naturally, in the main they will be middle-class but there will also be some from factories and farms, the older classes, and the odd politician risen from them, who do not want their memories ground in the churn. So long as they don't burn down *learnings centres* or in other ways hinder *synergies*, there should be no need to form secret societies and meet under freeways at night. They will be tolerated as readily as society now tolerates the people who grow old potato varieties, or buy them in little health food shops.

Mission statements and vision statements

What is a mission statement?

A company without a mission statement is like an evangelist without the cross or a shaman without her spirit animal. The same goes for any other business, including government departments, schools and kindergartens, hospitals, funeral parlours and nursing homes, cafes, sports clubs and bikie gangs: any band of people gathered for any roughly common purpose. When we lose our way in the world and forget what we're here for, our mission statement reminds us. It tells who we are and what we believe. If one day we don't recognise ourselves in it, then we know that either we *have an issue with alignment*, or the thing is no longer any good and we should exchange it for a better one – just as we would with a mirror.

A mission statement defines your mission, and the reason you exist.

> Writing a Mission Statement for a Business, Charity, Sporting Group or Community Group can be one of the most challenging tasks a group of people have to do . . . A mission statement is simple a definition of your mission . . . You should believe your mission statement and follow it to the letter.
>
> 1 on 1 Personal Computer Training

> Your mission statement should be a clear overview of
> your company values and ideals. A well thought out
> mission statement can convey your business purpose
> and reason for existence to your customers, suppliers,
> employees and shareholders . . .
>
> www.businesslifesolutions.com.au

It does pretty well everything, especially if the verbs are
proactive ones.

> An effective mission statement is concise, to the point,
> realistic, operational, inspirational, informative, and
> even emotional. It is forward-thinking, positive, and
> describes success.
>
> USA Swimming

> Your Mission Statement Should:
>
> - Express your organization's purpose in a way that
>   inspires support and ongoing commitment.
>
> - Motivate those who are connected to the organization.
>
> - Be articulated in a way that is convincing and easy to
>   grasp.
>
> - Use proactive verbs to describe what you do.
>
> - Be free of jargon.
>
> - Be short enough so that anyone connected to the
>   organization can readily repeat it.
>
> USA Swimming

Never go anywhere without it.

> The mission statement should be referred to
> continuously. It should be present everywhere: on the
> letterhead, all communications, all brochures, and all
> official documents.
>
> Australian Institute of Sport

And remember:

> If you don't believe in your mission statement or you don't believe you can achieve your mission, then don't undertake it as your mission.
>
> I on I Personal Computer Training

For example, would BAE Systems say 'Our services are grounded in a commitment to delighting customers' if they didn't believe it, or didn't believe they could *achieve* such delightfulness? You don't get to be the world's biggest manufacturer of guided missiles by fooling yourself, do you? But delight is not mandatory. General Motors prefers *total customer enthusiasm*:

> We are working to create an environment that naturally enables GM employees, suppliers, dealers and communities to fully contribute in the pursuit of total customer enthusiasm.
>
> General Motors

Then there's *customer satisfaction*:

> To be the best Fast Food Hamburger Restaurant in terms of customer satisfaction in both product and service and individual restaurant profitability.
>
> Hungry Jacks

And this:

> To provide outstanding customer service and products, in which creates United's point of difference to continue with innovative developments of our fuel and retail offer.
>
> A local petrol station

What is the relationship between mission statements and KPIs?

How do you know you're growing if you don't make a mark on the wall? And what is the mark if not a *key performance indicator*? A KPI is a measure. Sometimes they are called *key performance measures* – just make sure you get the 'key performance' bit in, because that's where the science is.

Say you want to grow a big bicep. What's the best way to check your progress? One obvious way would be to measure it every Friday night before you go out. But better still, measure it against a KPI, like a grapefruit. Ask yourself: 'How is my bicep going in terms of this grapefruit?' That's what KPIs are – things to measure other things against, one thing in terms of another.

Of course, they must be appropriate things. If your mission is to be a jet pilot, a grapefruit will probably not be among your KPIs. Depending on what you are measuring and how you are doing it, KPIs might also be called *signs, gauges, markers, appraisals, evaluations, estimations, tests, judgements, inferences, guesses*. We could choose from these and another dozen words to describe our mission, but the world is complicated enough already, isn't it?

Here's an example of a mission statement using KPIs – except they're KPMs, in this case.

Key Performance Measure 1: To develop the Number 1 Chinese Restaurant in Townsville and Surrounding Area

Key Performance Measure 2: Use the Freshest Ingredients

Key Performance Measure 3: Booked Out Every Night

Key Performance Measure 4: Feedback from our customers will be 5 out of 5.

By having these key performance measures you will know whether your business, sporting group, community group or charity is meeting its mission.

Sample PowerPoint Mission Statements, www.l-on-l.biz

What is a vision statement?

As much as you need a mission statement, you need a vision statement. Think of them as your rod and your staff. They are like twins. They share the same DNA – your company's DNA. What good can come from your business goals if you don't have the means to find them? What good are wings to a bat if it can't find the entrance to the cave? It needs its sonar and you need your vision statement, unless you want your company to flap aimlessly about in the gloom. And this is just as true when it's a *personal vision statement*.

> Your personal vision statement guides your life. Your personal vision statement provides the direction necessary to guide the course of your days and the choices you make about your career. Your personal vision statement is the light shining in the darkness toward which you turn to find your way. Your personal vision statement illuminates your way.
>
> Susan M. Heathfield, About.com

That's okay when it's just you. But a company has obligations to more than one *stakeholder* and needs a vision that suits all of them.

> Q. How do you craft a strong vision for your company? . . . It boils down to communication. Sit with the stakeholders who will be involved in that vision; try to paint the big picture and exchange ideas.
>
> Every vision breaks down into tasks to accomplish

it. Every task needs to be assigned to someone and measured, and then you need a maestro on top who's orchestrating the whole thing.

Smart Business Online

Vision statements – like visions – should be expansive. Who wants an anal vision statement? Big, bold and heartfelt is the way to go.

> We're a company with vision and values. BAE Systems is a systems company dedicated to making the intelligent connections needed to deliver innovative solutions to our customers. We're a company with a proud tradition of firsts continuing to take part in making the world a safer place. Key to our business is our strategic vision and what the company employees value. Our vision is to be the leading systems company, innovating for a safer world.
>
> BAE Systems (The world's fourth-largest weapons manufacturer)

We are guided by integrity, innovation, and a *desire for a safer world*. Blackwater Worldwide professionals leverage state-of-the-art training facilities, professional program management teams, and innovative manufacturing and production capabilities to delivery world-class, customer-driven solutions.

Blackwater (The US State Department's biggest private military contractor)

Our vision is that this could be a 300- to 500-unit part of our overall portfolio if our thesis is right about the ability to position this as the vanguard of Burger King restaurants.

Russ Klein, announcing new Whopper Bar in Orlando Florida. Russ is Burger King's president of global marketing, strategy and innovation.

What is the difference between a mission statement and a vision statement?

A mission statement is a formal written statement. A vision can be a bit less defined, but is equally important for longterm development of the club.

'How To Develop a Vision and Mission Statement', USA Swimming

It is the business visionary who, having focused his passion on the mission of his business and created a mission statement, then seeks to formulate and implement his desired future with a clearly stated vision statement.

Don Midgett, author of *Mission and Vision Statements: Your Path to a Successful Business Future*

Mr Midgett's advice, or something like it, has been followed in all kinds of remote places. In Tasmania, for example:

During 2006–07 we reviewed the Department's vision and mission statements. Everyone in the Department had the chance to be involved through workshops conducted in Treasury's offices throughout the State. The result is a powerful vision and mission that differentiates Treasury from other organisations. Our vision statement is a description of what we strive to achieve — a picture of the future we seek to create. It enables staff members to clearly imagine where the Department is heading. •

Department of Treasury and Finance, Tasmania

How do you write a mission statement or vision statement?

It's harder than it looks, so put aside a few weekends and hold plenty of brainstorming sessions. Then, if you follow these simple steps, you should have something by the end of the month.

Developing the vision and mission statement can be a lengthy task to find just the right wording that sums up and communicates the vision and mission of the business in an inspiring, memorable and defined way. This template will assist you in working with your team to develop the statements. If you have difficulties in achieving a desired outcome then we recommend that you speak to your Business Architect and consider a facilitated workshop. However this will attract surplus charges . . .

With the list of adjectives that you have listed . . . begin the process of developing a statement that best describes the vision of your business. To assist in getting a start, try using the following:

'Our vision is _____'

. . . When you have developed a statement that you are extremely happy with, document the statement and save it as a file labelled 'Vision Statement Year 2003 (or current year)'.

Enact Business Architects

What do mission and vision statements express?

They express things called *values*. Remember, all great organisations (the Roman Catholic Church, the Dallas Cowboys, General Motors) – and great people (Jesus, Abraham Lincoln, Jack Welch) – have great values. For example:

To achieve our aim, we have established five guiding values:

Customers – Our Top Priority. We will delight all our customers both internal and external, by understanding and exceeding their expectations.

People – Our Greatest Strength. All our people will be encouraged to realise their full potential as members of the team.

Performance – Our Key to Winning. We will set targets to be the best, continually challenging and improving the way we do things . . .

Partnering – Our Future. We will strive to be the partner of choice, respected by everyone for our cooperation and openness.

Not tolerating unethical behaviour by others, reporting unethical behaviour which we encounter, ensuring that our products are safe to use is a key responsibility. We also need to make systems as accurate as possible, and minimise the potential impact of our products on the environment . . . Lead used in ammunition can harm the environment and pose a risk to people . . . Lead free ammunition . . . will be available in 2005.

BAE Systems

According to the *Guardian*, since 2003 the company has been under investigation by Britain's Serious Fraud Office, the Swiss federal prosecutor, and authorities in Austria, Tanzania, Romania, the Czech Republic and South Africa.

Our corporate leadership and dedicated family of exceptional employees adhere to essential core values — chief among those are integrity, innovation, excellence, respect, accountability, and teamwork.

Blackwater

Blackwater has been the target of at least four grand jury investigations and accusations of tax fraud, improper use of force, arms trafficking and overbilling.

As an agricultural and technology company committed to human rights, we have a unique opportunity to protect and advance human rights. We have a responsibility to consider not only how our business can benefit consumers, farmers, and food processors, but how it can protect the human rights of both Monsanto's employees and our business partners' employees.

Hugh Grant, chairman, president and CEO of Monsanto

Monsanto is among the world's biggest agribusiness companies and the world's leading manufacturer of genetically engineered seed for food crops. An aggressive lobbyist and litigator, it has been sued for bribery and for damage to public health and the environment, and is frequently accused of dangerously misleading marketing and ruthless treatment of its workers and suppliers.

As you can see, mission and vision statements allow you to use your imagination. Here's a very imaginative one:

we believe . . .
life comes from life.
the soil is alive.
plants and flowers are living.
life is ever-present and recurring.
that life is in our products.
our products are very much alive,
the moment that they touch your skin.
life from life.

we believe . . .
beauty comes from beauty.
beauty is not processed. it is not made in lab.
it is grown and cultivated and cared for passionately.
it is not artificial. it is as real as our bodies and our
skin.
beauty is not always perfect, but in its imperfection, is
beauty.
we take beauty from the earth's unspoiled sources,
we bring that beauty alive in our products,
onto our skin, where it gives us beauty.
beauty from beauty.

Jurlique

But most mission statements just stick to the same routines.

Our core competencies distinguish the company from
other service providers and include . . . building and
maintaining added value partnerships that deliver
consistent service quality . . .

GSL Australia

Network PR connects people who matter to them.
With passion and precision we create networks
of influence, enabling clients to manage their
reputations, build their brands and enhance their
relationships with stakeholders.

Network PR, Wellington (New Zealand)

What are the essential words for mission and vision statements?

While it is true that no two organisations are the same, their mission statements tend to be. There is a good reason for this. You don't want words that set people thinking; or obscure words like *turgid*, *fustian*, *platitudinous* or *ornithyrincus*; or weird things about keeping your head when all about you are losing theirs or giving one's last full measure of devotion. You want plain, everyday words, such as *innovative*, *relevant*, *flexible*, *accessible*, *cost-effective*, *high-quality* and *products*. For example:

> Providing vocational education and training (VET) products and services that are innovative, relevant, flexible, accessible, cost effective and of high quality.
>
> Bendigo TAFE

> 4. That we achieve a comprehensive quality education through innovative and challenging teaching methods, a relevant, flexible and challenging curriculum and the use of a wide range of resources.
>
> Saints Peter and Paul School, Kiama

Then there are words like *engaging*, *clients*, *stakeholders*, *improve* (*continually* or *continuously*), and *customer service*:

> Engaging with our clients and stakeholders to continually improve our relationships, products and customer service.
>
> Bendigo TAFE

A lot of people like to sprinkle capital letters here and there.

> Stakeholders are the life blood of our organisation. We are Committed to providing our Stakeholders with Professional, Efficient and Reliable Standards.
>
> Eco Facilities Management

Then there's *integrity, honesty, ethically, deliver, promise, trust*. Just think about it – before mission statements, people could not rely on the honesty of organisations. Organisations could not rely on their own honesty.

> Integrity. We act honestly and ethically in all of our dealings and we deliver what we promise.
> **Bendigo TAFE**

> Integrity is the foundation of all that we do.
> **Monsanto**

> We believe in honesty, trust and integrity . . . We recognize that honesty, trust and integrity form the bond that holds organizations and relationships together. We are committed to open and honest communication.
> **Bogota Latin Bistro, Brooklyn, NY**

Safe, vibrant, sustainable, community, committed, improve and *partners* are all good mission statement words – especially *vibrant*.

> To provide a safe, vibrant, sustainable community while striving to constantly improve the quality of life for our citizens and economic partners.
> **'Members alter vision for future of Winchester', www.winchesterstar.com**

> Tumbarumba Shire will be a vibrant, caring, safe, secure and progressive community with a vigorous economy, where residents experience a good quality of life in a beautiful and sustainable environment.
> **Tumbarumba Shire Council, New South Wales**

> To be a vibrant, attractive and thriving District by developing sustainable lifestyles based around our unique environment; the envy of New Zealand and recognised world wide.
> **Whangarei District Council, New Zealand**

Commitment, outstanding, rewarding, risk managing – everything for everyone.

> We are committed to providing outstanding care for our patients, rewarding careers for our staff and achieving sustainable growth.
>
> Western Hospital, South Australia

> . . . a safe, rewarding, environmentally sustainable workplace in which all staff are encouraged and enabled to enhance their skills, develop their careers and realise their full potential.
>
> Centre for Excellence in Enquiry-Based Learning Strategic Plan, University of Manchester

Don't hold back.

> The Lorne Community Hospital is committed to achieving the highest standard of care for all clients, patients and residents. This commitment extends to the safety and security of our clients groups, their visitors, our staff, our suppliers and our community. We will maintain these standards through OH&S activities, Risk Management techniques, Quality Improvement programs and consumer participation in all that we do.
>
> South West Alliance of Rural Health, Victoria

> The DSSRM makes a strong effort to maintain a safe and secure conducive environment to allow educational, professional, and personal growth for all members of the school division and community where diverse social, cultural, and academic values are allowed to prosper.
>
> Stafford County Public School Division to the Department of Safety, Security & Risk Management, US

Outcome, strategies, achieve:

Physical Activity Policy Template

[INSERT SCHOOL NAME] Physical Activity Policy [INSERT DATE]

INSTRUCTIONS (DELETE WHEN POLICY IS FINISHED) REVIEW THIS 3 PAGE TEMPLATE. CONFIRM THAT OUTCOMES & STRATEGIES ARE APPROPRIATE FOR YOUR SCHOOL OR AMEND AS REQUIRED . . .

NSW Government

Outcomes, missions and even *strategies* are to be *achieved.* As in:

In order to achieve the Mission Statement, procurement must be central to the Council's business and operational decisions from the point at which the public service outcomes the Council wishes to deliver are identified, through the lifecycle of the requirement and the review of the delivery of those outcomes following implementation.

Highland Council Procurement Strategy

Transforming each function to achieve the strategy.

Goldratt ('Knowledge that delivers')

Benefits management to achieve strategy.

Victoria University Wellington, New Zealand

Processes are set up to help the company to achieve the reason it exists. Therefore process[es] are helping the company to achieve strategy. It therefore makes sense to align to strategy as the process underlines the strategy.

TechRepublic

And don't forget *passion* and *delight*.

> Innovate, execute better and faster, with more passion than any other . . . A passion to delight our customers, achieved through the delivery of superior quality, dependable on time delivery & service and partnerships built upon excellence and openness.
>
> Amcor Glass Australasia

> We will delight our customers by delivering a great experience.
>
> Synergy

> We will delight all our customers, both internal and external.
>
> BAE Systems

> These core competencies deliver value for all our stakeholders and enable the company to delight customers.
>
> GSL Australia

> A passion for our customers delivered through dependable on-time service, superior quality and partnerships built upon excellence.
>
> Amcor Glass Australasia

> Our passion is to exceed every client's expectations.
>
> Creative Folks

> Our Passion fuels Your Success.
>
> Hidden Pond

Mission and vision statements at work

Town mission

To accomplish that mission statement, the Comprehensive Plan lists seven goals, and according to Dreyer, the city has made accomplishments in each of those areas in the past year. Once the town has come up with a long-term plan it is possible it can receive more funds to implement them. Dreyer said it was premature to discuss what will be contained in the mission statement. 'It's going to be pretty broad and it will cover everything.'

Evening Sun, 28 January 2009

Private mission

Her personal mission statement helped her clarify what was important to her; to be there for her children, to be her best for her husband, and to be a role model of health and fitness for her children. Being a private person, Liz elected a different approach but established goals, armed herself with solid nutritional information, and hired a personal trainer to keep her on track.

'HOMEFRONT IN FOCUS: Living the Life You Want, Part 2', www.kitsapsun.com

Church mission

The church has built a four-part mission statement promising to worship with joy, grow in their faith through discipleship, care for each other through fellowship, and serve one another by sharing. It might sound like an easy job but the tasks the people are taking on are both large and time consuming.

'St Paul's United Methodist looks to future', www.chronicletimes.com

Fashola mission

What also can I say of this worthy successor of the worthy predecessor? Fashola has done well because he has a vision, he has a mission statement, he knows where he is going and where he wants to be. He understands that Lagosians may be facing some hardships now but he knows that nobody comes out of the hospital operation theatre without wounds, but the patient gets healed thereafter. Governor Fashola is equally making serious statements in other areas but time will fail me to recount all of them. Time will tell.

'On A Mission To Save Lagos', www.ngrguardiannews.com

Downtown mission/plan/vision already

'If you're going to launch a space satellite or if you're going to revitalize downtown, you've got to have a plan,' said Councilor Walt Skowron. 'I don't really see a mission statement. I'm looking for a mission statement.'

'Downtown Loveland revamp could cost $22.5M-plus', www.reporterherald.com

How do I write my *personal* mission statement?

As with anything that's going to change your life forever, you need to be in the right frame of mind. Begin with some simple stretching exercises or ten minutes on the exercise bike. Remember, you are about to transfer an element of a theory of organisations to you, an individual of astonishing cognitive complexity with 10 billion neurons in your cerebral cortex alone. It's a bit like cloning a sheep to a fence post, and you can't expect to succeed at the first go.

- Keep it simple, clear and brief. The best mission statements tend to be 3 to 5 sentences long . . .

- Think about how your mission affects the other areas of your life. Is it consistent with your other personal mission statements? Will it conflict with or contradict something else? Is it balanced?

- Make it emotional. Including an emotional payoff in your mission statement infuses it with passion and will make it even more compelling, inspiring and energizing . . .

If you are having trouble getting started, choose one of the sentence templates (whichever one appeals to you the most) and copy it into your word processor; then erase the '. . .[ ]. . .' parts and read the sentence from the start.

When you get to a gap, pause for a moment, and then let your mind fill in the gap. Just write whatever pops into your head.

www.timethoughts.com

Guiding principles represent your core beliefs, values, principles or ideals that guide you towards your mission/vision.

Some people like to use a prioritized list of values with short descriptions of how they want to live each value through this area.

Others prefer to use short quotes or maxims that represent an important principle.

Most people like to have three to five guiding principles for each of their life areas. You can use as many as you like, but don't go overboard or they start to lose significance . . .

Click here to signup for the free productivity start-up kit . . .

www.timethoughts.com

Other tips for writing mission and vision statements

Think of what you do in your business, then write the opposite. For example:

Respect, Integrity, Communication, Excellence.

Enron

We treat others as we would like to be treated ourselves . . . We do not tolerate abusive or disrespectful treatment. Ruthlessness, callousness and arrogance don't belong here.

Enron

Think about what you do, then write about diversity:

Diversity is at the very core of our ability to serve our clients well and to maximize return for our shareholders. Diversity supports and strengthens the firm's culture, and it reinforces our reputation as the employer of choice in our industry and beyond.

Lloyd C. Blankfein, chairman and chief executive officer, The Goldman Sachs Group, Inc

Our commitment to diversity is therefore unconditional; it is what we must be.

Lehman Brothers' mission statement

We have found that companies that have a written vision and values statement have a far greater Return on Investment than those that don't.

Jeff Skilling, president of Enron, All Employee Meeting, April 1998

Jeff Skilling said that in 1998, and Mr Skilling was no less than the president of Enron. Mission and vision statements are practical business tools, you see.

So avoid free verse and, no less strenuously, rhyme and meter. You are not writing an ode. No Latinisms. None of this sort of thing:

> diversity is the chore
> at the core
> for our clients
> to get more . . .

> what we must be
> we must be unconditionally
> committed to diversity
> as the English are to tea . . .

> we fish in fen water
> without a strategy and
> our boardrooms are stalked by slimy rats
> and eels . . .

Culture

Culture isn't something you can grow overnight – not a business culture, at least – and in general you can't do it by yourself. It's a consultant's job, really, and because cultures should be *diverse*, very often it's not just one consultant, but several. What is culture? It's all your *learnings*, *behaviours*, *values*, *actions*, *ideas* and *effortings* rolled together; and what the consultants do is explain it all to you *in terms of going forward* and then put in the *structural enablers* and *communicate the vision*.

Obviously, if you're running a knackery you don't want the culture of a high-end lingerie shop, though you will find that many words – especially *innovative* and *diverse* – do just as well for both. You have to find out what your own culture is, and then decide if it's the best one for you. You might like a *high-performance culture* or a *user-friendly culture*, or even a *culture of performativity*. While *diverse*, *flexible*, *innovative*, *tolerant*, *customer-focused* and *transparent* are the most popular kinds of culture and get the best press, *ad hoc*, *secretive*, *brutal* and *greedy* have also been known to work.

Culture reality scan

High Performance Culture Process

The process starts with a reality scan to assess the

organisational climate and culture. From the reality scan you can now define your current reality and design your case for change on a strategic staircase, which will assist you to achieve the future intent.

www.ihpconsulting.net

Sub atomic particles of cultural power

'Corporate Power' comes from consciousness, which is the sub atomic particle of culture. It is made up of thoughts, beliefs and emotions which are inherent in an organization.

Corporate Power is the sum of the collective consciousness of individuals in the organization, derived from organizational CULTURE.

Corporate Power, a consultancy group and affiliate of Deakin University, Victoria. Victorian government departments are among the company's clients.

Groundbreaking culture fit to strategy

We are living in complex times where doing the same thing well may not be enough. Our goal is to help you leverage culture to drive your strategy and achieve new levels of performance. With deep research into culture fit to strategy, an array of innovative diagnostic approaches and a team of organizational culture change experts, we can help your organization leverage its unique culture for future success.

www.culturestrategyfit.com

Flexible culture

Join us and you'll be part of one of the world's largest brands. You'll experience a culture of flexibility, opportunity, equality and diversity.

McDonald's Ireland

Try this one at home

Any shift to a high performance culture can incorporate a planned and/or emergent approach to organizational change that, in either case, would include these critical action steps for moving forward:

1. Identify the one or two cultural attributes that are most essential for long-term success and focus attention on them. As progress is made in that area, attention can be turned to other cultural attributes . . .

2. Communicate the vision of the desired culture in all available communication mediums including the informal channels.

3. Establish structural enablers of behavior consistent with the desired culture. At the same time identify and remove barriers that are preventing such behavior from occurring.

4. Establish structural barriers for behaviors that are associated with the undesirable culture.

5. Assess progress toward the desired culture and refine the above actions.

Ross A. Wirth, PhD, www.entarga.com

Umbrella culture

Build the talent pipeline with required workforce capability . . . Talent management is under the leadership and culture umbrella of the change roadmap.

From a training session at Kimberly Clark Australia

Indifferent culture

. . . ethical challenges come about because of a culture of indifference or a set of behaviours that model a 'if only we had the time' managerial mindset.

Dr Attracta Lagan, national director ethics & sustainability services, KPMG

Team culture

The aims of the subject are to explain and critique
a range of contemporary theoretical perspectives on
adult communication management and team culture
in order to enhance educators' analysis of the role
of teams in specific organisations to achieve high
performance and for learning collaboratively in
organisational settings.

Adult Communication Management and Team Work course, University of
Technology, Sydney

Internal enterprise culture

Fostering and facilitating innovation, the intelligent
use of knowledge and an internal enterprise culture
which embraces change are critical issues for
universities and their libraries.

Paper, International Association of Technological University Libraries, Brisbane

Customer focused culture delivered with levers of change

The Levers of Change team will deliver strategies
that enable a customer focused culture by addressing
organisational issues identified in the culture survey
results as requiring priority attention (to address gaps
or pursue opportunities for excellence) and designing
leadership development and support strategies.

Definition of a project within the Organisational Change Program, Child Support
Agency Intranet

Engaged, committed, ongoing culture – for Criminal Justice

The OPP is committed to the delivery of the following
key business priorities:

Drive positive change and service delivery
improvements within the Criminal Justice System

Develop with our people a culture of engagement, commitment and ongoing professional development in order to deliver quality outcomes . . .

From the job description for Principal Solicitor, Office of Public Prosecutions, Victorian Government

Knowledge retention culture

Key factors for effective knowledge transfer

- attitudes and culture — in particular, a base of attitudes of respect and open valuing of the tacit knowledge that resides with individuals, combined with long-term building of a culture of knowledge retention . . .

Clayton and Fisher

Performativity culture

The neo-liberal tenets, underpinning these regimes of efficiency and supporting a broad decline in social policy, are understood as spawning a culture of performativity within the sphere of education.

Dr Amanda Keddie, in an article in *Curriculum Perspectives*, the journal of the Australian Curriculum Studies Association, September 2005

Everything is culture and culture is everything

A company's culture is its personality. It tells people how to do their work. It takes its signals from leaders. It underlies motivation, morale, creativity, and marketplace success. How do you manage it? . . . Because a company's culture affects everything in it — including profits — culture is the real bottom line.

www.companyculture.com

In terms of consumer trading down by price points

ALI MOORE: What about demand? How much harder are current conditions going to make the turnaround you're trying to achieve?

IAN JOHNSON (CEO of Foster's): I don't think it's going to make any difference to us in changing our culture. I don't think it'll make any difference to us in reshaping the wine portfolio, putting in place the strategies we need to succeed. Where it does — where it can make a difference is in terms of if there's any consumer trading down by price points through our category . . .

Lateline, ABC TV, 17 February 2009

When you have decided on the culture you need for your organisation and got your structural enablers and barriers in the appropriate adjacencies, don't just stand there and expect it to start whirring and glowing all by itself. This is not an irrigation system, it's a culture: these are people you are dealing with — 'our people' — and as people you must treat them. Not that you can use an actual whip, but certain special phrases can be just as threatening. Remember, we're not talking about the ballet but how organisations control their people — organisations like Telstra.

Hear the word culture and reach for your gun.

GREG WINN (COO of Telstra): We're not running a democracy. We don't manage by consensus. We're criticised for it but the fact of the matter is we run an absolute dictatorship and that's what's going to drive this transformation and deliver results.

It's a cultural issue. If you can't get the people to go there, and you try once and you try twice, which is sometimes hard for me but I do believe in a second chance, then you just shoot 'em and get them out of the way you know and put people in that you can teach the new business process to and drive on.

Four Corners, ABC TV, 18 June 2007

Poor adherence

DEBBIE NASH (former Telstra call centre consultant): Adherence is a schedule. You have to be on time, you have to go on breaks where they have set a break for you, and if you're on a phone call with a customer, that can affect your adherence adversely, and you can be, you know, penalised at the end of the month for that, for having poor adherence.

Four Corners, ABC TV, 18 June 2007

Help me understand – or will Boris break your legs?

JOHN ROLLAND (Telstra customer sales and service executive): What it was setting out to achieve was to let leaders understand the impact they have on others, particularly the people that are reporting to them; and how they needed to respond in their role as coaches and as leaders.

'JANELLE' (former Telstra call centre team leader): You would be very direct with them, like, 'Help me understand what you're going to do to meet your targets by the end of the month.'

QUENTIN MCDERMOTT: Is that a particular phrase?

JANELLE: 'Help me understand' was a very popular phrase, very popular.

Four Corners, ABC TV, 18 June 2007

Performance improvement path

QUENTIN MCDERMOTT: Tell me about the bottom line.

JANELLE: Well, the bottom line is this, Quentin: you either pass your scorecard or you or we go onto the performance improvement path — that's the bottom line.

QUENTIN MCDERMOTT: It's essentially a disciplinary process, isn't it?

JOHN ROLLAND: No, it's an improvement process to help them get the skills they need to achieve at their job.

Four Corners, ABC TV, 18 June 2007

Balanced scorecard

QUENTIN MCDERMOTT: What happens if they don't achieve the targets?

JOHN ROLLAND: We continue to work with them.

QUENTIN MCDERMOTT: And what happens after that?

JOHN ROLLAND: If a person who joins us over time is not able to achieve the balanced scorecard that we've got — and it's not just about sales; it's about customer service and other issues — then we will have a discussion about them finding other opportunities outside Telstra.

Four Corners, ABC TV, 18 June 2007

Eliminate dragons

JOHN ROLLAND: Dragons, in particular, are the things that hold us back from achieving what we want to achieve as leaders.

JANELLE: If I was looking at putting someone onto a Performance Improvement Plan, the dragon for me would be the union delegate.

Four Corners, ABC TV, 18 June 2007

Ditto submarines

QUENTIN MCDERMOTT: Submarines, tell me about submarines.

JANELLE: Well, if you've got a group of twelve people in a team, you don't want anyone flying under the radar and not performing, you don't want those submarines.

Four Corners, ABC TV, 18 June 2007

And all negative behaviour

QUENTIN MCDERMOTT: There's another extraordinary term isn't there — savages?

JANELLE: Yeah . . . You can have savages in your team, and they were actually referred to as people that have got negative, perceived to have negative behaviour that doesn't benefit the team, so they're a savage.

JOHN ROLLAND: The call centre business is not for everybody and we respect people's choices if they no longer find that work compelling, to make the choice to leave, and Sally made that choice.

QUENTIN MCDERMOTT: Sally Sandic left Telstra at the end of December. Less than four weeks later, she committed suicide.

Four Corners, ABC TV, 18 June 2007

Values

Values are . . . the things you value. Except your money. Or any synonym for money. Values, bless them, are never concrete. If what you value most is lobster thermidor, don't worry: you don't have to put it in. The same goes for canoeing with your mistress or World Championship Wrestling. A lot of those things will be filtered out in the team-building exercises.

If you're not sure what your values are, or indeed if you have any, drill down until you reach the time you were a boy scout. Remember the oath? The stuff about truth and honesty? That's all you need. Don't drill any further: you never know what you'll find. Come to think of it, the safest way to find your values is to get them off someone else's website. Throw in innovation, diversity and teamwork, align the whole thing with your business goals, and away you go – synergised.

Aligned values

> She is a proven chief executive whose values are closely aligned to the Westpac culture.

> Westpac announces its new CEO

Heart and soul values

> We . . . are working with the Advisory Group to look at new ways of representing our values. We agreed that the best way to commence with this Heart and Soul project (Heart and Soul is a new market for us to capture) is to seek your advice and collaboration . . . I would like to request your positively inspired thoughts on 'creating a better world in which to work and live' and what this means for you.

> An email (A Value Proposition and Request for Your Engagement) from a corporate communications manager

Framework of values

The Unilever community is shaped and led by its people, who operate creatively within a framework of shared values and business goals.

'Our People', Unilever Australia

Render the following as a haiku or rhyming couplet.

Surface the values

Know how to use the curriculum to facilitate cognitive and experiential learning as logical stimuli to surface the values involved.

'STAR Program offers abstinence centred sexuality teaching for teens', an article in *Family Update*, the newsletter of the Australian Family Association, March–April 2006

Translated values

Policy is a mechanism for the translation of the priorities and values of the organisation into programs and practices to deliver outcomes.

Government definition of policy

Sit down, look ahead, revisit and realign values – and get everyone on board

In response to requests by service providers, the team has been supporting organizations to sit down with service users, families, boards and staff to start looking at the task ahead. For most organizations, the best place to start is to get stakeholders together and revisit the organizations mission and core values and realign on purpose and direction. Having achieved this, the next step can be to look at the standards and identify examples of practice for each, then start to identify policies and procedures that need to be in place (or updated) to support these good practices. This exercise not only gets everyone *on board* from the beginning (an important part of meeting the standards in itself) but it creates *a plan for action*.

Queensland Branch, ACROD, National Industry Association for Disability Services

What?

. . . GOVERN OURSELVES THROUGH A VALUES-DRIVEN PARTNERSHIP

- Live by the principles of an involved partnership
- Benefit from individual freedom and assume the obligations of mutual accountability and self-governance
- Maintain a meritocracy
- Operate as one firm

Omni Consulting group

Enhance your enjoyment of this account of Treasury values by reciting them aloud with a friend.

Fun and supportive, passionate treasury values in a values-based environment and culture – a celebration

Everyone in the Department was involved in the selection of Treasury values that were launched in a Department celebration on 15 July 2005 and since then our decisions and behaviour have been guided by the following values and belief statements:

Integrity . . . as it builds confidence, trust and self-respect, and is the foundation of open and honest communication;

Excellence . . . as it challenges us to give our best and brings us recognition;

Respect . . . as it recognises the value of each of us and the contribution we all make;

Camaraderie . . . as it creates a fun and supportive place to be; and

Passion . . . as it inspires us to achieve great things.

In addition to the belief statements, we have developed some core behaviours to help us apply our values. Each branch and work group has supplemented these with its own set of behaviours to help guide workplace behaviour and decision-making in line with our values, mission and vision. The behaviours are reviewed regularly to ensure that they are still valid and meaningful.

We want our staff to put the values into practice. The values team has identified a range of additional initiatives to support and instil our values throughout the organisation . . .

During the past year Treasury has implemented a Leadership Development Framework to help develop the type of leaders who are comfortable operating in a values-based environment and who recognise and support our values-based culture.

Department of Treasury and Finance, Tasmania

The Monsanto Pledge. Read this slowly and think of golden fields of corn. Ask yourself challenging questions as you go: what else might the Monsanto Pledge compel people to do? What else might integrity include? What else might transparency ensure, sharing knowledge advance, and innovative science deliver? Etc.

The Monsanto Pledge is our commitment to how we do business. It is a declaration that compels us to listen more, to consider our actions and their impact broadly, and to lead responsibly. It helps us to convert our values into actions, and to make clear who we are and what we champion.

Integrity: Integrity is the foundation for all that we do. Integrity includes honesty, decency, consistency, and courage. Building on those values, we are committed to:

Dialogue: We will listen carefully to diverse points of view and engage in thoughtful dialogue. We will broaden our understanding of issues in order to better address the needs and concerns of society and each other.

Transparency: We will ensure that information is available, accessible, and understandable.

Sharing: We will share knowledge and technology to advance scientific understanding, to improve agriculture and the environment, to improve crops, and to help farmers in developing countries.

Benefits: We will use sound and innovative science and thoughtful and effective stewardship to deliver high-quality products that are beneficial to our customers and to the environment.

Respect: We will respect the religious, cultural, and ethical concerns of people throughout the world. The safety of our employees, the communities where we operate, our customers, consumers, and the environment will be our highest priority.

Act as Owners to Achieve Results: We will create clarity of direction, roles, and accountability; build strong relationships with our customers and external partners; make wise decisions; steward our company resources; and take responsibility for achieving agreed-upon results.

Create a Great Place to Work: We will ensure diversity of people and thought; foster innovation, creativity and learning; practice inclusive teamwork; and reward and recognize our people.

The Monsanto Pledge

Put yourself in the other person's shoes – or else

Q. How do you make sure employees are living your company's values?

If you don't talk about it, it's not going to happen. Talk about it and have an open discussion of what these values mean to you. When people step over boundaries, get them to accept that this is the way you wish to be treated. Put yourself in the other person's shoes. If anyone is not making decisions or interacting with anyone in a way that does not live up to these values, then they shouldn't be part of the organization.

Smart Business Online

Living the no-brawling, crime or cocaine values

We have spent a lot of time developing this, talking to a lot of different people who are well versed in leadership structures, across the business world and other areas, to come up with a structure and program.

We believe this is a part of an action plan for change to move forward and be even better.

The key thing is showing strong leadership to achieve what we want to on and off the field, and those players have to be more committed to that than anyone else to lead the way.

The leadership group will be enforcing that, and living the values that are put in place.

West Coast Eagles coach John Worsfold and vice-captain Dean Cox, applying business principles to drug use, brawling and other 'hi-jinks' at the club

Aligning your values

From around the time of Aristotle to about 1995, philosophers pondered the question of values without understanding that unless they are aligned with business goals, they'll just fly around the office like so many blowflies. Set aside a couple of days to get them where you want them and allow at least a month for *buy-in* – then sit back and watch your people. You'll see it in their eyes first: the self-possession, the sense of purpose growing to unstoppable, hyperNietzschean zeal. They'll be on rails, like little locomotives with your brand embossed on all their boilers.

Regular review is essential. You don't want to find yourself with a pledge to 'Act ethically at all times' when your business goal is a little outside the parameters of that particular box. This is when you realign: 'Act flexibly at all times' might be a better alignment in the circumstances; or 'Try to act ethically' or 'Be innovative in all that we do'. Of course, you always have the option of keeping the values and dropping the business objectives – but what are you in business for? Your values?

Aligned with Jesus

There is a strong Catholic identity and witness to Christian values, ensuring that our Mission, shared beliefs and our core values align with the person of Jesus Christ.

Sacred Heart College, Geelong

Misalignment

Know your people. If you're trying to reward someone, something that you enjoy to do after hours might not be the same that the employee enjoys. If I give them a ticket to a baseball game, yet they don't like baseball, what are they going to get out of it? You've got to know what they do and enjoy, and try to align with that.

Smart Business Online

Core alignment

Q. How do you determine the core values of your employees?

Core value alignment. Don't tell them your core values, but ask probing questions that will get them to talk about things that they've experienced. Ask them about a situation in their business experience that challenged their integrity, and get them to talk about it. You will be able to determine their core values based upon questions you ask them. If you told someone, 'Here are the three core values of our company; does that align with you?' they'd be crazy not to nod their head and say yes.

Q. How do you make sure employees are aligned with your vision and that you are living it each day?

By their actions. Just look at their actions and ask yourself, 'Does this truly align with the vision that we have here, and is it going to be healthy for the company?' Execute what you're preaching. Get feedback from others, unsolicited feedback as to what others see as your core values and what you're thought of as a leader. Separate the person from the issue, and don't attack the individual giving you feedback.

Smart Business Online

Continuous Catholic improvement

At Sacred Heart College we have adopted a culture of continuous improvement with a structured approach to curriculum, professional development, pastoral care, resourcing and master planning . . . We are a dynamic school community that embraces and incorporates change that is consistent with our values.

Sacred Heart College, Geelong

Aligning what we say with what we do

A truly customer-centric organisation will have a strategy that conspicuously reflects a commitment to addressing what our customers are telling us, ie it is about getting what we say and commit to doing aligned with what we actually do and ensuring that this incorporates customer requirements.

Chief Customer Service Officer, Centrelink (PowerPoint presentation)

A chain of critical mass

We partner to our strengths combining your organisation's merits and aligning goals to create a chain reaction of critical mass along the same path of success; therefore meeting your expectations and fulfilling our Mission Statement.

Meritocracy Partners

Passionate, wise alignment

Our Mission Statement

When we all have a PASSION for what we do and can TRUST each other, we create ALIGNMENT and become equally RESPONSIBLE for one another. Powertech has adopted the universally accepted hierarchy of understanding to create alignment from a top down approach in everything we do.

The hierarchy demonstrates the relationship between Data, Information, Knowledge, Wisdom and Understanding. Not only does this hierarchy give rise to all Company principles, policies, procedures and proformas, it is also the foundation for our core values which embrace four key concepts:

* Passion
* Trust
* Alignment
* Responsibility

Powertech.com.au

Sensemaking alignment followed by afternoon tea

Communication Framing and Stakeholder Alignments in Intractable Environmental Conflicts (followed by afternoon tea)

This presentation focuses on the communicative framing of intractable environmental conflicts. It reviews the different approaches to framing and focuses on framing as a communicative process in which the disputants reveal their sensemaking about five aspects of conflicts. The presentation then centers on the homogeneity and heterogeneity of stakeholder framing in these five categories across four different conflict sites.

Seminar at Griffith University Brisbane given by Linda L. Putnam, Professor of Communication at Texas A&M University

Endeavouring to behave

This Statement aligns to Council's core values, primarily through the value of 'Openness and Accountability'.

In keeping with this value, Council will endeavour to behave with integrity, impartiality, transparency and fairness at all times.

Nambucca Shire Council

Attunement

In this paper we extend Swanson's (1999) model of attunement and her proposition that executives' receptivity to values is key to aligning corporate behaviour with broad-based expectations of responsible conduct. Our extension of her model is threefold. One, we underscore the importance of identifying values relevant to attunement. Two, we point out that pressure from special interest groups can constrain an executive's inclination to foster those values that serve the collective good. Three, we propose that 'trustful dialogue' can help align corporate conduct with the needs of the community at large.

Marc Orlitzky and Diane L. Swanson, in an article titled 'Theory of Socially Responsible Executive Decision-Making', *Australian Journal of Management*, 2002

Commitment – a definition

Commitment is about being willing to do everything necessary to reach an outcome so long as it is in alignment with our values even if it is to our personal cost. Being committed means being willing to act in spite of fear. It means being willing to do what is hard. It means knowing that each of us alone can choose to succeed in spite of any barriers that may be put in our way.

www.lenkayeenterprises.com

Good alignment

Hawkesbury-Hills Division of General Practice's Mission Statement is 'Advancing General Practice in North West Sydney to optimise health and wellbeing in our community'. Hawkesbury Division of General Practice's mission and values show good alignment with the identified national health priorities . . . All activities within this plan have been checked against these values and fulfill at least one, and in many cases multiple, value/s.

www.phcris.org.au

Executive alignment

Our Objective

Is to impact business growth and development through implementation of learning and development solutions that identify Executive Values, Align Values to Drive Motivation and Change, and so provide all stakeholders in the Enterprise, a transparent competitive edge. TMOA is a human resource management consultancy, which services a variety of corporate clients in addition to assisting the development of smaller businesses.

www.tmoa.com.au

Learnings

Learnings are what you have learned. In the olden days they called them 'lessons' and said things like, 'What did you learn at school today, Geraldine?' But now we say *learnings* and things like, 'What were your learnings at school today, Geraldine?' or 'Did you get any learnings from the Learning Centre today, Nicholas? Any *key* learnings, lad?' Learnings are sort of mental outcomes. The other thing you could call them is *knowings*. We don't say 'knowings', but if we did, knowings would be stuff we just sort of know – like our shoe size or what a kiwi is – and learnings would be stuff we learned in team-building, or something. The other thing is that learnings are lifelong. Learnings never end. That's why we like to present them in fun activities.

Bendable pirate learnings

Key Learnings for Corporate PR Fall 2008

Bendable Pirate Characters. As our fall semester is winding down in my Corporate PR class at Georgia Southern University, we had a fun way to wrap up the key learnings. Each student chose a small character (ninja, pirate or rubber ducky) from a basket and named the character. Then they each came up with a word or phrase that started with each letter in the name. (Full directions to the assignment are at my Becoming Learner Centered blog.) A few volunteers came to the front of the class and presented their key learnings to us by showing their list and character on the document projector. You'll see what the key learnings for my students were as comments to this blog post. By having them create their own mnemonics in class today, I'm hopeful that they'll remember many of the key points of this class long after it is over.

www.publicrelationsmatters.com

Shared learnings

In an effort to spread the corporate learnings and stay accountable to the six-month timeline, conference calls were held every other week with the corporate team lead . . . First, each hospital administration designates an eMAR coordinator to serve as a single point of contact to facilitate improved multidisciplinary communication for shared learnings across the corporation.

www.psqh.com

Video learnings

It got me thinking, 'What are our key learnings about video as a livelihood option for the poor?'

www.pbs.org/idealab

Deep learnings

You know, they say it's not how you fall down; it's how you pick yourself up. I think many learnings in life don't come from the easy days, they come from the difficult days.

Stuart Lawson of HSBC Russia

Delightful learnings

Anne Marie Smith is a global expert on integrating governance into processes and methodologies, with many years of experience from both academic and practitioner perspectives. We're delighted that she's sharing her learnings with us.

www.prlog.org

Key learnings

Key Learnings for Insurance Companies on How to Manage Their Reputation.

www.ipsos-ideas.com

Adult learnings

Learnings for Adults.

Dr Shailesh Thaker's 'Top Management Blog – Asia'

Leveraged learnings

Working in the corporate world has always leveraged my learnings from all aspects.

From a blog

Benchmarked learnings

Any learnings are taken over for the critical part planning phase of the next cycle and industry benchmarking.

www.logisticsmagazine.com.au

Assimilated learnings

Thereafter, the team needs to assimilate its learnings and add it to the organisation's knowledge bank.

www.gulfnews.com

Applied learnings

It's highly relevant and the modules are bang up to date and I am applying learnings to my day-to-day job.

www.econsultancy.com

Echoing learnings

I appeal to you to echo your learnings in this seminar to your peers in your offices or in your organizations. Let us continue to operate with a positive mindset, can do attitude and competitive spirit. Let us keep the momentum of change and progress. Our successes have multiplier-effects especially to nation building. We have done much, but we can do much more.

I am confident as you are that we will hurdle the challenges and push our city to a higher ladder of competitiveness

Vice Mayor's Closing Remarks, Seminar on Seven Key Drivers of Competitiveness, Shoe Hall, Marikina, Philippines, 22 September 2006

Just another learning

That's just another learning we'll have to take away from the match.

Michael Voss, football coach

Meritocracy

This lends your outfit (not to say yourself) a bit of class. The idea is that talent and effort should determine who gets the power and rewards in the organisation. It sounds fairer than nepotism or croneyism, to be sure, but then again, power is power and an elite is an elite, and the chances are you'll end up with a powerful elite as smug, obnoxious and self-serving as any determined by heredity or money, and one with worse dress sense.

Michael Young, the man who came up with both the word and the theory, thought meritocracy a danger to civilisation; but people who love the market love the meritocracy. They love the word as much as they love the whole idea, and they don't give a fig what an old Englishman thinks. This might be because meritocracy is nicely aligned with their fat bonuses and makes them feel like Darwinian heroes at the same time. The more the market works for them, the more they confuse the theory of meritocracy with the one relating to the divine right of kings (minus *noblesse oblige*, of course).

There are some other little questions. Who decides what is meritorious and what is not? How do you measure merit?

How do you stop those who win the power and rewards deciding these matters in their own interests or the interests of school friends and cronies? And who is to say – *vide* Wall Street, meritocrats to a man and woman – that the people capable of rising in a system are in the best position to judge whether it's a good system or not? And if it's so much better than the old hierarchies, how come the years of meritocratic fashion have given us a society in which wealth is *less* equally distributed?

It's a naughty world, that's what it is, and whatever works for you is probably the best idea. Meanwhile, spare a thought for those who don't make it to the top: in the old days they could tell themselves it was an accident of birth, but now there's nowhere to hide – they are minions because they are meritless. Still, they have the company values to make them feel wanted.

Terminate, terminate

Unless it's in your mission statement to employ underperforming staff, make a commitment to a meritocracy culture in your firm . . . Meritocracy does not tolerate deadwood. A standard of performance is established, below which (after developmental efforts have failed) employees are systematically terminated . . .

Omni Consulting Group

Congenial meritocracy

To do this within a congenial, meritocratic working environment that rewards industry, creativity and entrepreneurialism and gives KM people purpose as well as employment. To maintain market agility and an open-minded and international approach to all business and people issues while continuing to expand operations.

Human Capital Magazine

Wir sind meritocrats!

The absence of meritocracy creates disillusionment and failure. We must find ways to mobilize employees around the firm's vision, to then achieve alignment with, and commitment to those central values. We must develop a leadership mind-set that embraces meritocracy as a vital force in how we improve our firms, and lives.

Omni Consulting Group

Obligation free assessment of merit

We invite you to call 1300 MERITS for an obligation free consultation. Our selection process allows for the engagement of those projects, which fulfil all stakeholder requirements as we only take on a limited number of cases to best allocate the resources to succession.

www.meritocracypartners.com

The origin of realtors

Be part of the 'Evolution' team.

We are creating something special and are looking for winners.

Founder and Managing Director Ian Barnes has an impressive proven track record of success, understands what it takes to create a winning culture, how high achievers think, and what their needs are. Evolution Realty has a huge vision. We have taken a long term view of our mission as real estate giants in our markets and to add value to our respective communities . . .

If you want to be part of an exciting new opportunity to make a difference and excel in an environment that rewards results, initiative and hard work and practices meritocracy, then we want to talk to you. Join us at Evolution Realty.

www.evolutionrealty.com.au

So much for merit

'The PR challenges were far more relevant than I thought they would be,' he said. 'I thought we operated in a meritocracy.'

'Founder, CEO of Blackwater Steps Aside, "Worn Out"', *The Wall Street Journal*, 2 March 2009

Team-building

Team-building teaches people how to *share the vision* and *live the values and the brand*. And how to speak the same language. It *embeds learnings* and *improves the bottom line* for paintball manufacturers whose market would otherwise be limited to children, early teens and rugby players. Team-building breaks down our people's resistance to change. It breaks down the barriers between them. It breaks down some people altogether and for good. Team-building means fun activities that can give your people the sort of unconquerable sense of belonging that part of an earlier generation got from walking alpine trails singing 'The Happy Wanderer', or it can give them the sense that they have been consigned to a re-education camp or nursing home.

The stored experience

The experience provides a common language, experience and story, which can be related to the work environment. The experience can provide a short cut in communicating a shared vision very quickly. The experience is stored in a way that is able to permit participants to see themselves and their colleagues in a new light. The experience (and stories attached thereto) can serve as a catalyst for continuing the theme in the organisation.

From the experiential learning research of corporate psychologists Dr John Luckner and Reldan Nadler

Fairly general

[Team-building] is a fairly general term that is used in a number of different ways. It can cover either what you are trying to achieve and how you are trying to achieve it — or both! . . . The definition that we prefer is: Improving team performance by developing teamworking skills by using any appropriate method. It is a fairly general definition but encompasses all of the normal definitions.

www.teamwise.co.uk

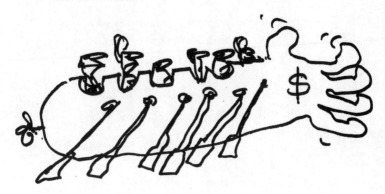

Imprinted whole body learnings

Teams are able to experience chaos, disorder, crisis and changing requirements for success in a safe environment where the consequences for failure are limited. The team can develop strategies and best practices for managing these issues both in this environment and back at work . . . Experiential learning is an anchor for cognitive material. Participants have a kinaesthetic imprint or whole body learning of cognitive principles because the learning is graphic as it involves physical, mental and behavioural dimensions.

From the experiential learning research of corporate psychologists Dr John Luckner and Reldan Nadler

TBI

Team Behavioural Inventory (TBI)

Team Behavioural Inventory is an inventory or checklist of positive and negative behaviours associated with team high-performance and based on the team wheel.

www.argospress.com

Combat zone to raise the bar and focus

Build a strong, agile, high performance team. THE COMBAT ZONE program combines the best elements of the outdoors into one great TEAM adventure. At the completion of the program teams feel a deep sense of achievement, self-confidence, camaraderie and satisfaction in what they have accomplished.

Does your team have power, confidence within and trust to follow through? KENDO, is the most powerful and exhilarating event your team will experience. Using the ancient ways of the Samurai warriors and the art of Japanese Sword Fencing, individuals are taken on a journey that tests their commitment, building self-trust, raising the bar and focus.

www.teambuilding.com.au

Drill down to behaviour

'We drill down and look at any problems upfront — at different examples of where a type of behaviour is being exhibited,' Turner continues.

www.personneltoday.com

Capital fun

On one away day, according to sources, Abrahams came on to the platform dressed in a Las Vegas showman's costume. Behind him were a series of props hidden behind sheets. One was an electric chair. As he strapped a director in, he had the line from the rock song that goes 'I hate you and I hope you die' playing. It was part humiliation, part making the point that anyone who gives away Barclays' secret 'know-how' on these deals would get it.

The Guardian, 20 March 2009

Better health outcomes for animals

One vet spoke of her anger and frustration after 130 staff from the Midlands Animal Health division attended a training day in Warwickshire on Tuesday (10 March). The vet had expected the training to be focused on the latest strategy for tackling bovine tuberculosis. 'Instead we wasted an entire day playing games, mucking about and banging drums,' she said . . . A spokeswoman for Animal Health rejected the vet's claims. 'As well as strategy, aspects of the day focus on effective teamwork and how it can help Animal Health deliver better outcomes in the future.'

Jonathan Riley, www.fwi.co.uk

Great platform for meaningful connection

During dinner the activity can be framed to discover
key skills, talents, and insights about the talent at the
table. Each person has a question and they interview
the person on the right and left. This creates a great
platform for meaningful connection. This is a great
springboard into a discussion for the coffee/dessert
portion to share the direction of the rest of the event,
share the vision/plan/agenda and ask how knowing
these insights into the team will enhance/accelerate
the learning experience and application ability when
they get back to their roles. Ask them to share what
they discovered, what was new, and how it impacts the
future they are all looking at.

Discussion thread, www.peak-adventures.com

Forging the divides

So the sales representatives donned full-length
paintball armor and were divided into two teams
that, curiously, followed the same pecking order that
had polluted the office in the first place. 'The event
had successfully forged the deep personal divides
we'd hoped to dissolve,' said Garvey, who would have
preferred some open dialogue and tequila shots.

Jared Sandberg, *The Wall Street Journal*, 7 January 2007

Bond or die

Team-building proponents counter that winning
requires working as a team and communicating
loudly. 'If they don't work as a team, they get
shot and experience pain. It's not for everybody,'
Roberts said. 'But the principles of communication,
teamwork, leadership and strategic planning are
there.' . . . 'Learning is sometimes optional from their

perspective,' admits Roberts of clients who sometimes aren't looking to improve performance. Still, he is big on debriefing and follow-ups. Even if they aren't fond of it, 'a lot of bonding happens' among people who think it is ridiculous, he said.

Jared Sandberg, *The Wall Street Journal*, 7 January 2007

Waterboarding for salespersons

No one really disputes that Chad Hudgens was waterboarded outside a Provo office park last May 29, right before lunch, by his boss.

There is also general agreement that Hudgens volunteered for the 'team-building exercise,' that he lay on his back with his head downhill, and that co-workers knelt on either side of him, pinning the young sales rep down while their supervisor poured water from a gallon jug over his nose and mouth.

And it's widely acknowledged that the supervisor, Joshua Christopherson, then told the assembled sales team, whose numbers had been lagging: 'You saw how hard Chad fought for air right there. I want you to go back inside and fight that hard to make sales.'

What's at issue in the lawsuit Hudgens filed against his former employers — just as in the ongoing global debate over the CIA's waterboarding of terrorism suspects — is the question of intent.

Karl Vick, *The Washington Post*, 15 April 2008

A great learning about life

We all learnt that the only failure in life is the failure to participate and came away as a team of people who are focused on clear outcomes.

A dental company newsletter, summing up its recent Vision Conference

Horses for bankers

[I enjoyed] working with horses and being at a ranch to experience team building outdoors.

Dario Yanez, Wells Fargo Bank, www.paramountperformance.org

Tipi building for bankers

Our team of senior managers really liked the tipi building and felt they learned something about themselves and others. I have recommended this experience to our Events Department.

Eloise Jones, Wells Fargo Bank, www.wasatchadventure.com

Fascinating

The S.T.A.R. Profile

This is a quick and fascinating way to find out about yourself and each of your team members. The S.T.A.R. profiler was developed at Corporate Games, Inc. to illustrate how people differ in terms of Styles and Tendencies, Abilities and Reactors (what motivates each individual).

www.corporategames.com

The advantages of being a 'challenge and innovate' kind of person

A 'Challenge and innovate' employee 'builds on others'' ideas, encourages and owns implementation of ideas.

A 'Trust and Team Spirit' employee 'instils pride and passion in team achievements'.

New performance criteria for staff at the Commonwealth Bank

Cascading horror

If you wish to play an office prank on your colleagues then just try walking into the office and mentioning in passing that there is a company team building event planned soon. The looks of horror will cascade around the office as your colleagues picture the trust falls and group chanting in a secluded field somewhere around Dorset . . .

www.content4reprint.com

Customer experience

Experience before *customer experience* was hardly worth having. Of course, there are still people out there who remember when a nice man in overalls put petrol in your car, cleaned your windscreen and checked your tyres, battery and radiator; when banks had managers who met you in their offices and would never have expected you to conduct your private business among the cheerful multitudes at the teller queues; when you could buy your rabbits off the back of a truck. Well, that was the experience of customers, but it wasn't *customer experience*.

The old kind of customer is going the way of the nightman and chicken chow mein, and their memories are going with them. Soon the only kind of customer experience will be the kind you get when *everyone's* a customer: when the preferred experience, if not the only experience, is *customer experience*; when to be alive is to be a customer and to be a customer is very heaven . . . etc.

Delight breakpoint v patience threshhold

The company considered raising service levels to the 'delight breakpoint' or reducing them to just above the 'patience threshold.' Customer-lifetime-value economics pointed to the second option: relaxing service levels but guarding against crossing the patience threshold. The drop in customer satisfaction was negligible, but the savings in staffing were significant, and the company ended up saving more than $7 million annually.

From 'Maintaining the Customer Experience' by Adam Braff and John C. DeVine, *McKinsey Quarterly*, December 2008

Actionable insights into addiction

A second source of strategic and tactical help is my book *Addicted Customers: How to Get Them Hooked on Your Company*. This book was written before the recession but what it provides is actionable insights into the psychological principles that lead to emotionally compelling customer experiences.

John I. Todor, 'The Perfect Customer Experience' blog, December 2008

Customers into advocates

In designing propositions for specific segments, leaders focus on the entire customer experience.

They recognize that customers interact with different parts of the organization across a number of touchpoints, including purchase, service and support, upgrades, billing, and so on. A company can't turn its customers into satisfied, loyal advocates unless it takes their experiences at all these touchpoints into account . . . To ensure effective delivery, the leaders must first create and motivate cross-functional teams — from marketing to supply chain management — to deliver their value proposition across the entire customer experience.

The Three 'Ds' of Customer Experience

The perfect customer experience is one which results in customers becoming advocates for the company, creating referral, retention and profitable growth.

Dale Wolf, 'The Perfect Customer Experience' blog, 2006

Unique and exceptional

. . . You will provide unique and exceptional customer experience, oversee childcare services and assist in growing membership sales. You will drive a high performance culture with team coaching and development . . .

Job advertisement, 2IC Health & Fitness Manager, Western Sydney

World class experiential master

Following the webcast, we will share how you can receive a copy of this research report (no registration required), 'The Customer Experience Maturity Monitor: 2008.' This report details the trials and trends, and provides a benchmark for companies to measure where they stand in the race for a world class customer experience. In this study, we introduce five levels of maturity ranging from 'Limited Capability' to 'Experiential Master' and explore what it takes to move from the base of the continuum to the peak.

www.bettermanagement.com

Non siloed

Treat customer experience as a competence, not a function: Customer service is everyone's priority, not just that of the contact center. Call it 'customer experience,' 'customer advocacy,' 'customer insight' – anything, Temkin pleaded, that avoids dumping it into a siloed department.

Jessica Tsai, 'The 5 Levels of Customer Experience Maturity', 29 January 2009

In-store

Successful retailers will embrace new communication and marketing models to respond to market segment preferences and ensure in-store customer experiences provide a differentiated value proposition relative to alternative emerging retail channels.

Rodney Baurycza, Telstar marketing manager

Contentment

Customer Experience – A focus on planned, consistent customer experiences that embody the Centrelink brand and lead to optimum outcomes in terms of customer contentment, costs to Centrelink and Government, and improvements in customer circumstances (reflecting desired policy outcomes) . . . this has been an engine room for innovation across our network . . .

From Centrelink Future Directions 2004–2009. Centrelink's customers are people receiving social welfare.

Hot muffin experience

The 'Storm Model' hinged on luring potential investors to initial group education sessions, where they were sold the benefits of the Storm approach. Like everything in the Storm empire, the fine detail was important. Thousands of dollars were invested in muffin warmers and top-of-the-line coffee machines to have fresh smells wafting through conference rooms when potential clients arrived. Many were given a tour of the offices, to underline for clients the message that they too could share in this wealth. 'The whole new customer experience was like nothing on this planet.'

Eric Johnston and Vanessa O'Shaughnessy, *The Age*, 17 January 2009

Leveraged voice of the customer

'We are enabling more people around the business to get their hands on the data. It's about creating value around that and value for the business,' he said. 'We are enabling businesses to leverage the voice of the customer in order to give a better customer experience.'

www.vnunet.com

Some enchanted customer

BU1006 — Managing the Customer Experience

This subject is about designing, assessing and managing the interaction between customers and business. It introduces students to a number of approaches to customer experience, a term which helps define the experience economy. In the experience economy successful businesses must orchestrate memorable events or 'experiences' for their customers. The subject uses this new paradigm as a basis for understanding traditional and emerging worlds of business. Concepts relevant to managing in the experience economy include time management, mindfulness, servicescapes, enchantment and satisfaction studies.

James Cook University, School of Business

The missile customer is always right

Strategic Capability Solutions focuses on the development of transformational capabilities, technologies and processes, designed to deliver continued business success and shareholder value for BAE Systems and more agile, flexible and cost effective solutions to the Company's customers.

BAE Systems

Customer experience experienced

Valued Customer

Dear Valued Customer,

During the year the key cost drivers of our industry — commercial property prices, transport and labour have continued to rise. Whilst we have absorbed some of the rising costs by way of operational productivity improvements, it has been necessary to review our pricing . . . We are confident that you will appreciate the responsible approach we have taken to the pricing review. Should you have an queries with regards to the new rates, please do not hesitate to call our Customer CARE team . . . Recall thank your for your continued support and recognition, and appreciate your understanding of this necessary price increase.

Recall

Terminated customer

Thank you for your call. The anticipated waiting time for this call is longer than we would expect you to wait. In appreciation of your time, patience and cost implications to yourself, we are terminating this call.

Driving Standards Agency, United Kingdom

Customer as hero

For over 70 years, Motorola has been incorporating the latest technologies into practical, progressive solutions for real situations and rigorous environments. We hear the call and answer with innovative, high quality tools for mission-critical heroes.

www.btw.com.au

Customer with escalated issue

Dear Ms. Chipman

I note your dissatisfaction and understand your frustration in regard to the issue raised.

Ms. Chipman, I have escalated your concerns to the relevant department for a feedback. Please be assured that you will be contacted at the soonest possible time when a feedback is received.

Your patience and understanding in this matter is highly appreciated.

From Nokia

Customer in different point in time

. . . it has been through a rescheduling process from the previously planned point in time to a later point in time . . .

www.weaselwords.com.au

Another customer with a point in time issue

With respect to your enquiry as to when the system will be available to you again; we advise at this point of time, we have no definitive date with respect to when this functionality will be restored.

A Unisuper online message

Customer on hold

We have placed your application on hold within our system . . . The estimated completion date is TBA, however this date may be moved forward or back depending on demand and availability of equipment.

From a Primus Telecom letter to a valued customer

Otis regrets

To enhance the performance of the vertical transportation at 222, Exhibition St, we wish to advise that the lifts are going through a re-adjustment program. Please excuse any inconvenience that the process may contribute to the lift services during this period.

Otis

Realigned for everyone's good

As part of our commitment to our clients we are realigning your client management team to further service your current and evolving needs and to strengthen your relationship with us.

Bank letter

Operationalise the value proposition in terms of product sets

So you start with the research, the needs based research, you go in and you group into segments and then from the segments then you can start developing value propositions. Value propositions segment by segment by segment by segment. Because the key then, and again the big differentiation, is what do you do at that point? How do you operationalise this notion of these value propositions? And the way I think about it and the way I've done it in the past is you execute it in terms of the product sets and applications and services by segment. You operationalise it by the channels that you use to interface with those customers. You operationalise it by the service experience that the customer wants.

Sol Trujillo, CEO of Telstra; Trujillo's annual compensation package was $8.7 million

Driving everything we do

Our aim has always been to help our customers reach their destination on time and without fuss, in a safe, comfortable environment and it drives everything we do. We focus on consistency in logistics and safety, and clear communications to make travel easier. We respect our customers' time is precious and continuously drive innovation to improve the quality and value of our services. We believe by making an ongoing commitment to these challenges, and by acting with integrity doing what we say we will do we are able to build certainty into train travel for the people of Melbourne . . .

Melbourne train operator Connex, which in June 2009 was fined $11.2 million for poor performance

Invitations, commitments, thank you each and every one of you

As a valued customer, you are invited to accept our invitation . . .

A bank's offer to increase credit limit

If you walk into the supermarket to buy a ready-to-eat meal for that evening, we want to make sure we are engaging you in a softdrink offering by communicating it to you . . .

A business magazine

We invite you to have a look at our deliverables on human factors in our website.

Eurocontrol

We want to personally thank you for submitting Microsoft your suggestion.

Automated webpage

People

Hiring our people (and dehiring them)

No business can hope to succeed if it just drags in any old wretch off the street and parks them in front of the knowledge desk. A successful business must be flexible, diverse, innovative, customer-focused, inspired by its mission, guided by its vision, empowered by its values, governed by its strategy, aligned with its goals, living by its brand, driven by its drivers and all but consumed by its desire for continuous improvement going forward – and so must the people who work for it.

For a wide-ranging outcome

Those in charge of recruiting and selecting new staff face a decision-making process that needs to be responsible in its implementation and to produce a positive and wide-ranging outcome.

Corporate Power

Deliverable driver (commercial)

. . . you will govern the strategic planning of the 'F Block' project and be responsible for driving the commercial deliverables of the project development phase via management and co-ordination of a multi-disciplinary team.

East Browse Business Opportunity Manager Senior Leadership Role at Shell

Target audience engager and identifier, etc.

In this role you will be responsible for a range of
activities including identifying and engaging target
audiences, building and maintaining productive
relationships with various stakeholders, and providing
strategic advice on embedding knowledge and
adoption principles and activities in all stages of
research.

Land and Water Australia

Solution architect

The purpose of the Solution Architect role is to lead
strategic design, scoping activities and support the
implementation of information solutions that meet
organisational plans, needs, and functions, and assure
their alignment to enterprise goals and the overall
IS architecture. The role has primary responsibility
for maintaining and deploying the Enterprise
Architecture, with particular emphasis on Technology
Infrastructure and the Security Framework.

New Zealand District Health Board

IAAM (reporting to IAM)

The Information Assurance Architecture Manager
reports to the Infrastructure Architecture Manager
and will lead a small section taking on architectural
and coordination responsibility in the area of
Information Assurance and Technical Security.

Department of International Development, United Kingdom

Product evangelist

Cinegy, a Munich-based developer of enabling IT tools, such as codecs, asset management and workflow solutions, has named Martin Libich to the newly-created post of Product Evangelist for North America.

www.cinegy.com

Director of leverage, integration, alignment and fostering

The Design Leverage Director will be an important, contributing member of the senior management team and will have accountability for leading the integration of design thinking across the organisation, aligning design principles with business strategies that enhance operational performance and fostering a collaborative, innovative culture that generates creative solutions.

Corporate Project Office, Australian Customs Office

Ambiguous change manager

Dear Bill,

Thank you for your email. I appreciate that our advertisement for this particular role was ambiguous. Essentially, this is a new role for Customs at the Senior Executive level and is a role that will require the incumbent to use design theory and design thinking as an agent for organisational and cultural change and will champion best practice project management processes and procedures in a complex environment. We are looking for someone with a proven record in leading strategic change management and project management initiatives in large, complex organisations, coupled with outstanding relationship management skills.

Corporate Project Office, Australian Customs Office

Strategy translator (executive)

Executive Assistant to the Executive Director, office of the Chief Executive

Reporting to the Director, Human Capital, you will leverage your background in selection and workforce planning to translate our business strategy into our people strategy to ensure that we have the 'A players' in the right roles with the right skills at the right time.

Manager, Human Capital, at www.careerbeacon.com

Deliverables driver and achiever

Provide high value management to the Lean Six Sigma Team by developing and maintaining systems and driving Portfolio and Black Belt deliverables necessary to ensure appropriate governance . . . Manage and coordinate strategic and tactical processes for the deployment of Lean Six Sigma throughout Asset Management Group to achieve deliverables within the Program . . . Optimise the deployment of Lean Six Sigma resources at all levels by effectively managing the mentoring process and its outcomes for Black Belts and Green Belts.

Program Coordinator, Railcorp NSW

Interpersonal humility

Excellent interpersonal skills, including a sense of humility.

IT Director qualification

LPA

Loss Prevention Associate.

Position vacant sign at the Glenfield Mall (Auckland)

Team-builder

Essential for this challenging position are high level management and leadership skills and a demonstrated capacity to perform effectively under pressure and in the face of conflicting demands. There is a strong focus on team building . . . Career opportunities at Villawood and Baxter detention centres. GSL are justly proud of our reputation and values. It is our people's commitment to excellence and innovation that will make GSL a great company.

GSL (Australia) Pty Ltd

Vibrant dental atmosphere

DENTISTRY WITH A DIFFERENCE

Are you looking for a work environment where people come first?

Where excellence in empowering communication and co-operation is valued as highly as clinical competence?

Where all staff are encouraged and free to be both independent and interdependent?

Where the atmosphere is vibrant and questioning; and the search for better ways of helping people is always on? . . .

Do you see every person as a unique individual, wide and deep?

Do you feel honoured to be a dentist? Are you looking for an exciting change of direction?

Would you consider joining a team with meaning? We would love to hear from you.

Job ad

Quality learning outcome achiever

Reporting directly to the Head of Learning Australia you will present true consulting expertise across specific internal client groups. Working closely with these key stakeholders, you will provide solution leadership management to ensure the achievement of agreed strategic and business objectives between Learning and the business. Building effective and constructive relationships you will pro-actively engage and advise the business to achieve quality learning outcomes.

A job advertisement on www.seek.com.au

Credit decisioner

. . . Provide assistance to direct reports on the development of strategies to structure and decision credit proposals.

Risk executive, Commonwealth Bank of Australia

Fun job at the Tax Office

We seek a director to lead our team. You will develop and implement strategies to deliver outcomes from the perspective of our clients and act as an advocate for the client in our business lines decision making processes.

Change program, client and staff integration, Australian Tax Office

Content auditor for Content Integrity Team

Opportunities exist for motivated, quality conscious people to form the Content Integrity team . . . The Content Auditor will advise on the quality and accuracy of written and spoken content. Supervise the addition of new non-content provider created text to existing content and services.

www.seek.com.au

Temp

'Non ongoing position'

www.weaselwords.com.au

Champion adherent of the absolutes

To assist the Maintenance Manager in implementing and
developing a preventative maintenance and continuous
improvement system/culture for all our equipment and
operatives. Also to Champion preventative maintenance
and housekeeping, ensuring we set high standards
consistent across all operations and that we engage
buy-in from all staff . . . To strictly adhere to the
Absolutes issued by the Operations Director . . .

Continuous improvement/quality manager, Harrison Scott Europe Ltd

Ensurer (with additional responsibilities)

To ensure that the Commercial Manager is continually
updated on performance improvements in order
that we can improve our added value and/or be more
competitive in the market place . . . To ensure any
recommendations to Site Facilities are agreed with
the Maintenance Manager and that these are actioned
promptly within agreed timeframes . . .

Additional Responsibilities:

- Be a trained Fire Marshall
- Be an active member of the Business
  Continuity Crisis management team
- Be an active member of the Health & Safety
  Committee
- Be a trained Risk Assessor/Auditor
- Be an active member of the Environmental
  Team

- To present when requested at Company Presentations
- To hold a Institute of Leadership Management Certificate
- To be a Black Belt in Six Sigma or hold comparable qualification in Continuous Improvement

Continuous improvement/quality manager, Harrison Scott Europe Ltd

BRM (team-located)

Benefits Realisation Manager and measurement metrics

You will be located in one of the four Enterprise Capability Group teams. The Enterprise Capability Group is responsible for the identification and definition of strategic capabilities for Centrelink's future. (Location in this team will last approximately six months whereby the position will be transferred to the Enterprise Program Office.)

The successful applicant will:

- work with Investment Programs to facilitate agreement between stakeholders on the benefits to be delivered, assisting in the development of measurement metrics and monitoring the delivery of agreed benefits . . .

Canberra Times, 18 December 2004

Exemplary and Flexible Officer required for unpredictable library customers

Vital to success in this position will be:

- Exemplary customer service skills that reflect an understanding of the underlying principles embedded in Same Day Service.

- How well you demonstrate flexibility and adaptability working in an environment where the expectation is that the unpredictable will occur.

Library customer support officer, Community and Cultural Vitality Division at the City of Port Phillip, Victoria

★ ★ ★

Deliver is a word to precede *outcomes*, even outcomes of the most intangible kind – such as dreams: 'Parents and local communities working with our leadership and teaching teams in schools will help us to build high expectations, engage learners and focus teaching on delivering new dreams for our students and communities.' A few years ago, no minister for education could have hoped to get away with something as silly as this, but once people become used to *outcomes* being *delivered* all the time, soon enough they'll achieve *buy-in* with their dreams. 'There are those who look at things the way they are, and ask why . . . I dream of things that never were, and ask why haven't they been delivered?'

Excellent, creative, strategic, passionate and flexible – person

Excellent presentation skills; both written and verbal are essential as is the ability to be creative and strategic in your approach. Passion for entertainment products and a flexible work ethic is required.

National promotions manager – entertainment

Faciliator/interfacer

Reporting to the director, the role facilitates the work of the HR functions, continuously improves strategies and procedures, whilst interfacing the internal and external environments.

Manager – administration, Monash University

Mandate to leverage

Your mandate is to leverage your clear, insightful understanding of operational performance into the implementation of practical initiatives that improve business outcomes.

Chandler Macleod

Negative stakeholder manager

Does the candidate have proficiency in managing negative stakeholders impacting her own workplace situation?

Ernst & Young, doing a reference check

Fair, equitable, courteous, sensitive team leader

Role profile

Operate as the leader of a team, supporting employees; lead the achievement of that team's business outcomes. As a member of the office leadership team, achieve business outcomes which deliver high quality customer services in line with the Government's agenda, and lead the implementation of identified strategic priorities at the local level.

Duties

(1) Lead a team in the fair, equitable, courteous and sensitive treatment of customers within legislative and policy frameworks and to specified standards.

Centrelink

★ ★ ★

Quality job descriptions do not come easily to everyone. To save embarrassment, many organisations give the job to consultants expert in describing complicated manoeuvres with key verticals and key players in particular spaces.

> My client is a global player in their field and as such they are truly looking for the best of the best caliber candidates for this role and their company. This role involves conducting research on key verticals and identifying and contacting key players within that particular space.
>
> Cool and funky conference producer / people seeker, Time Recruitment

Passionate and talented group seeks credible relationship-builder

Engagement Consultant x 3

This is an exciting opportunity to join this passionate and talented group that is genuinely committed to people investment and development. As a progressive and dynamic leader, our client is dedicated to continually build and develop people capital.

Tertiary qualified in Education/Learning, you have a specialised L&D/OD background and experience in all aspects of the learning process. You build credible relationships, have strong influencing and consulting skills and enjoy working within a dynamic and progressive environment.

Seek.com

Newly identified position for a key member

This newly identified position will report to senior site management and support the Group Manager Stakeholder Relations, to maintain and enhance trusted and valued relationships with external and site stakeholders. As part of this key role, you will develop and implement effective communication strategies to provide quality and timely communications to all stakeholders along with participation as a key member of the business Stakeholder Relations Network.

Media Relations, My Career.com

★ ★ ★

When considering job applications treat the jargon with a dose of salts – or a grain of salt if you're old fashioned. Whatever gets up your goat less.

I specialize in the implementation of workplace solutions that leverage self-directed teams toward increased throughput.

Quoted in 'Cover Letter Gaffes' by Kevin Donlin, www.careerowlresources.ca

Never call them 'staff'. They are human beings. But don't call them that either. Call them 'people', as in: 'Our people set us apart from the crowd.' They are always 'our' people, but try to make it sound more like you love them than own them. Westpac does it really well:

Our people play a key role in Westpac's involvement in the community.

Westpac

These are just two examples of how we put the rhetoric – 'our people are our greatest asset' – into practice.

Westpac

We're offering our people the chance to develop a Collective Agreement that suits them and suits our business.

Kate McKenzie, group managing director of wholesale, Telstra

Our people are talented, energetic and motivated to continually expand their knowledge and improve their performance.

American International Group (AIG)

I'm just really concerned about the safety of our people.

Edward Liddy, CEO of AIG, speaking to the US House of Representatives

A CEO is a priest and his people are his flock. And a priest . . .

We will give our people opportunity to learn and dialogue on these topics of concern . . .

Mission statement, St Paul's Lutheran Church of Teaneck, New Jersey

Saying vamoose to our people

Because we value our people, we are committed to letting them down gently. We can't call them family one minute and the next talk as if they're a discontinued product line. There are many ways to say goodbye; but don't we owe more than 'Ta ta' to our fellow human beings?

Right size by staff balancing

Ford in Australia will 'right-size our business' by 'staff-balancing changes', according to chief executive

Marin Burela. 'We would be taking proactive steps in terms of reducing our throughput through our build operations . . . In line with the production down-balance we have also taken the opportunity to take a good look strategically where we are, what we're doing and how do we move forward.'

The Age, 16 October 2008

Streamline the back-end

800 jobs will be lost as Telstra streamlines its back-end office functions.

www.slatteryit.com.au

Down balance with personnel implications

As I said we're studying that now but we believe that the personnel implications of the down balance will be in the region of 300 to 350 employees.

Sinead McAlary, Ford Australia spokeswoman, ABC radio

Impact by a reduction – respectfully

Everyone impacted by this reduction deserves our thanks and respect for their contributions to the company . . . This realignment will allow us to increase investment in high-growth areas of the company . . . [We] look forward to a bright future as a company if we can execute on this vision.

AOL email to staff

Refresh the team

Three of the most senior staff in the Planning Department have lost their jobs in a reshuffle insiders say is clearly aimed at giving developers more sway over government policy . . . The executive

director of the taskforce, Aaron Gadiel . . . said
yesterday he was pleased with the changes, saying
'there's nothing wrong with teams refreshing
themselves from time to time'.

The Sydney Morning Herald, II May 2009

Enhance the management structure

Please be advised that A and B left the Company last
week, after a carefully considered decision was taken
to pursue an enhanced management structure in the
Contact Centre.

Email to Fairfax staff, 29 July 2005

Unavailable to work – as such

Peter Lloyd has been sentenced to 10 months in prison
in Singapore today on drug-related charges, and as
such the ABC's employment relationship with Peter
has come to an end. This is due to the fact that Peter is
unavailable to work.

ABC Corporate spokeswoman, 2 December 2008

Upgrade with immediate effect

We are going to upgrade you with immediate effect.
We are going to allow you to move on in order that you
can you use your talents and skills more effectively and
thus upgrade your career and opportunities.

www.ftd.de

Synergy-related headcount reduction

With the successful completion of these plans, we will
have the vast majority of the synergy-related headcount
reductions completed and we can then start to put this

chapter of our history behind us and focus on creating a world-class company.

Nokia Siemens Webwire, November 2008

Commitments to diversity, etc., are not impacted by the implementation of these processes.

Change management

For a long time in human history nothing changed, at least nothing that needed *change management*. Then, about twenty years ago, everything began to change. And – lo! – a whole new industry was born, and a mighty lode for consultants revealed. Armed with the *knowledge* and the *tools*, the evangelists moved across the continents dispensing learnings unknown to all previous generations, along with colourful mouse-pads, beanie dolls, screensavers, posters, movies and invoices, all bearing the message and the company logo. Not that it's so simple you can manage without a consultant.

> 'I do change management with an unusually high degree of involvement from the stakeholders, so that there's ownership, so that the whole thing is sustainable, so that people jump for joy at the initiative and all the stakeholders in the company actually make it work,' he said.
>
> www.thetimes.co.za

Change management defined

> The first and most obvious definition of 'change management' is that the term refers to the task of managing change.
>
> Fred Nickols

Useful factors

To define the purpose it is sometimes useful to
consider input factors, throughput or process factors
and output and outcome factors.

Queensland Health change-management documents

Typical change management practitioner

A Change Management Practitioner has mastery of
the change principles, processes, behaviours and skills
necessary to effectively identify, manage, initiate and
influence change, and manage and support others
through it.

Definition: Behavioural Competencies
Clusters of behaviours that are related to success in
a given role.

www.change-management-institute.com

The Tasmanian model

It should be noted that the Tasmanian Government
Project Management Framework stipulates that
Departments frame Business Case funding requests
and Project Business Plans in terms of the business
drivers rather than solely technology or infrastructure
requirements. In this sense, there are no 'ICT'
projects as such, but rather projects with business
drivers that may include an ICT component as part of
the solution.

www.epress.anu.edu.au

Identify resistors, including severe resistors

Change Management is an organized, systematic
application of the knowledge, tools, and resources
of change that provides organizations with a key

process to achieve their business strategy. Managed Change™ is the LaMarsh & Associates, Inc. approach to change management and is designed to bring the organizational and people sides of change together — for results and benefits. Addressing the human elements of change by way of this disciplined approach will increase the speed of implementation of your change project and thereby decrease the cost. Working through the Managed Change™ model, change agents identify the potential for resistance, why that resistance may occur, who could potentially be resistant, and the severity of that resistance.

www.lamarsh.com

Business continuity needed for business continuity

A managed process shall be developed and maintained for business continuity throughout the organisation that addresses the information security requirements needed for the organization's business continuity.

International Standard ISO/IEC 2700I:2005(E)

Resourcing up for the site gap analysis

Also as promised, I did speak to the High Performing Organisation Project Manager. She stated that the progress needs to be on bedding down the design prior to then going about any assessment or implementation. [She] mentioned that from a resourcing standpoint, currently it is only set up with 1.5 FTE to deliver the design work. Following the design signoff an assessment will need to be made around how to resource up for the site gap analysis . . . The purpose of the end user workshops is to validate and test the design . . .

Email from a change management advisor to Coles Myer Ltd

Corporate Social Responsibility (CSR)

After the rorts, scandals, failures and near failures of the deregulating 1980s, CSR became the mandatory new business wisdom, as indispensable to the company profile as the mission statement. Smart companies – and those best placed to actually practise a bit of CSR – saw that it was good business to add good citizenship to the brand.

While some went no further than tacking a bit of egregious fizz about ethics and integrity to the mission, others talked about *sustainability* and *diversity* as though they were suddenly *core business* and the community were part of the main game. They also talked about higher standards of *corporate governance* and becoming *employers of choice*, about extended maternity leave, childcare and career paths for their employees – and about how such values were *part of their DNA*.

Some noticed that the fashion among governments to sell public assets and place public services in private hands had left private-sector companies, including corporations, with unfamiliar quasi-governmental powers and responsibilities. The CSR document was born of the need to reassure citizens (or *customers* or *stakeholders*, as they became) that this revolution had cost them nothing of much importance. Their rights, their security, their environment, their money – nothing had changed except the brand.

Often CSR sounded like a management version of the broadcast from the ransacked palace when the bodies have been taken away; at other times it was like the Sermon on the Mount, as a football coach might have written it. The company task was made much easier by the frantic efforts of a much-diminished public sector to rearrange itself on the private-sector model. Public- and private-sector organisations took the same advice, engaged the same consultants and, of course, parroted the same reassuring slogans. 'Our shared core values of honesty, integrity and respect for people, underpin all the work we do ...' etc.

Some of the private companies really did become better citizens, even if the flatulence of *all our stakeholders, customer-focus, transparency, accountability* and *our people* made it hard to believe them. Of course, you can lay on CSR with a trowel and still go on doing business with nothing but the bottom line in mind. Or you can ignore the whole thing. A lot of people won't like you, but your shareholders won't always be numerous among them, and in following your free enterprise instincts and sparing us the baloney you'll also spare yourself consultancy fees.

An ethical company

> BAE Systems recognises its responsibilities to the people it employs, its customers and suppliers, its shareholders, the wider community and to the environment. We are a well-managed, responsible and ethical company and are determined to be widely recognised for our world-class technology, the skills of our people and the seriousness with which we take our corporate responsibilities.
>
> **BAE Systems**

Associated Press, 1 December 2008: 'Switzerland can hand over bank documents to British authorities investigating whether arms manufacturer BAE Systems PLC bribed Czech politicians to gain a lucrative contract for the sale of fighter jets, the Federal Criminal Court said Monday.'

A more ethical company

> So we have all got to be aligned and ensure that our PPR objectives directly support our strategic goals. This process will start with the Senior Management Team and be cascaded downward through G&I ...

Additionally, our success also depends on our business execution — practicing personal accountability and discipline while delivering projects to our customers.

And most importantly, do not forget our focus on ethical standards exemplifying honesty and integrity in all we do.

Bruce Stanski, executive vice president, G&I –Halliburton

US Securities and Exchange Commission, 11 February 2009: 'The Securities and Exchange Commission today announced settlements with KBR, Inc. and Halliburton Co. to resolve SEC charges that KBR subsidiary Kellogg Brown & Root LLC bribed Nigerian government officials over a 10-year period, in violation of the Foreign Corrupt Practices Act (FCPA), in order to obtain construction contracts. The SEC also charged that KBR and Halliburton, KBR's former parent company, engaged in books and records violations and internal controls violations related to the bribery. KBR and Halliburton have agreed to pay $177 million in disgorgement to settle the SEC's charges. Kellogg Brown & Root LLC has agreed to pay a $402 million fine to settle parallel criminal charges brought today by the U.S. Department of Justice. The sanctions represent the largest combined settlement ever paid by U.S. companies since the FCPA's inception.'

As ethical as a company can be

Corporate Governance: Code of Ethics Introduction

Titan is very proud of its reputation for excellence and commitment to upholding the highest ethical standards. As always, Titan's ultimate success in both of these areas begins and ends with our greatest resource: our team of highly qualified and talented employees. All of Titan employees share certain core values.

www.titan.com

Titan employees were named in the US Army Investigation into the abuse of prisoners at Abu Ghraib. In 2005 the company admitted that it committed bribery for a telecommunications contract in Benin. For this and filing false tax returns, Titan settled with federal regulators, agreeing to pay $28.5 million.

The golden peacock

Satyam had in September (2008) this year received 'Golden Peacock Global Award for Excellence in Corporate Governance' from the World Council for Corporate Governance. A Satyam release posted on its website said: 'The honour is especially relevant given that corporate governance best practices are considered key benchmarks by stakeholders who evaluate corporations. In fact, their importance is magnified in difficult economic environments.'

www.economictimes.indiatimes.com

Reuters, 10 March 2009: 'The founder of fraud-hit Satyam Computer Services and four others have been sent to the custody of India's federal crime bureau for investigation into the country's biggest corporate scandal ...'

A CSR showcase

The Competitive Advantage of Corporate Social Investment: Developing Effective Corporate Community Engagement Strategies to Drive Business Performance.

Conference run by IQPC (International Quality & Productivity Centre)

Enhance the *Leadership Consciousness* in your organization. Select and retain powerful intergrated and wise Leaders, who know where to go, what to change and how to change to achieve sustainable ethical business outcomes, and who skilfully quickly and effectively harness people's hearts and minds in a common direction.

Corporate Power

How we manage our people will reshape the destiny of organisations . . . Our obligation to our shareholders and all stakeholders may be best met by effectively making each employee head of corporate responsibility.

John McFarlane, CEO of ANZ

CHICAGO – The National Automatic Merchandising Association will again feature a Corporate Social Responsibility Showcase at its Spring Expo and is calling for companies who want to share their sustainability efforts.

www.vendingtimes.com

During 2003 we have ensured our CSR activities are fully aligned with our efforts to deliver our key business objectives.

The CEO of BAE Systems

Consultants

What is a consultant? Think of one of those birds that ride around on the backs of cows. Think of dozens of birds on the cow, and on every bird another bird, and another bird, until you can hardly see the cow. Think of one of those little fish that attach themselves to whales, then do what you did with the birds. There are, of course, many differences between consultants and those fish and birds: one of them is that only consultants can manage to sound smug and ridiculous at the same time.

Feel free at any time to stop reading and set up a consultancy. Begin by composing a description of your services, along the lines of those that follow here.

End-to-end people solutions

With highly credentialed, real-world experienced, international recruitment teams applying robust, creative and thorough sourcing and assessment methodologies, the skilled and ambitious people that we deliver, sharpen organisations' competitive edge . . . Our HR Consulting team's passion and expertise lie in HRO, RPO, career planning, training management and psychological services. A tailored RossJuliaRoss HRO solution enhances the return on an organisation's people investment and frees up key resources in your internal HR team . . . RossJuliaRoss's end-to-end people, technology and process solutions address every stage of the employee lifecycle of a candidate.

RossJuliaRoss HRO

Leveraged Sage data

PROPHIX Software, a leading provider of financial business intelligence and performance management solutions specializing in forecasting, corporate budgeting, strategic planning, consolidation, financial analysis and scorecarding, is proud to be sponsoring a session in the Exploring Integration track at the 2008 Sage Summit. The session, entitled 'Leverage Your Sage Data for More Strategic Planning', will take place on Tuesday, November 18th at 3:30pm.

Press release

Product evangelist with MBA

I'm offering a service to become your company's product evangelist. I have an MBA and have built internet applications for events, directories, online publishing, and images as the product (marketing) manager. I've developed social media sites, and the biggest challenge is knowing which features to keep or discard . . . The lesson that I've learned is to get out and start evangelizing the product or service when there's a spike in churn or when adoption flatlines.

An advertisement on www.craigslist.org

Increased synergy

Through strategic alliances with other associations, APPA increases the depth and breadth of its information and offerings, broadens its scope and value, leverages its resources, and creates increased synergy across the facilities and educational community.

APPA – leadership in educational facilities

Removing inactive bananas

. . . to keep workplace essentials exactly where they should be, consultants have told civil servants to mark out spots for their pen, phone and computer keyboard with black tape . . . The edict also banned workers from keeping food on their desks and restricted them to one cup, pen and pencil. Fruit was allowed only if it was 'active' — jargon for whether or not it was about to be eaten. So-called 'inactive' fruit was outlawed. One worker had a banana on his desk and was asked whether it was 'active' or 'inactive'. He was told he had to eat it or remove it.

London Evening Standard, 4 April 2009

Future gold

Futures Alchemy: the fusion of foresight, insight and
creativity. Our futures intelligence work is alchemical
in nature. We take the raw ingredients for success; add
the revelation of foresight, the depth of insight, and
the spark of creativity that transforms the lead of the
present into the gold of the future.

Designer Futures

Executing the deliverables

Finally, the book sets out best practice tools,
methodologies and approaches for creating a strategic
tax plan, developing the enablers and executing the
deliverables.

PricewaterhouseCoopers

Executable strategy

Previous research and leading practices . . . provide
key metrics that can improve workforce productivity
and performance, they also enable their HR personnel
to translate human capital data into executable
strategy.

Unlocking the DNA of the Adaptable Workforce. The Global Human Capital Study
2008 Executive Summary

Solving human capital

We will provide human capital solutions with
intelligent workflow making your people more
productive, innovative & strategic. By partnering with
us your organisation will become more competitive,
profitable & valuable.

EmployeeConnect

Effective creative

Fresh is rejuvenated and ready to show you how our
Fresh solutions and effective creative can benefit your
business . . . Fresh can assist you to analyse and define
your brand goals, create and develop your new brand
and corporate identity, or reposition, redesign and
revitalise your existing brand to meet your corporate
strategic goals.

Fresh

Diversity recruitment skills

Our consultants possess a wide range of diversity
recruitment skills that can seamlessly integrate
with your organisation's consulting needs. We have
successfully developed policies, Toolkits, diversity
councils, survey analysis and general diversity projects
for some of Australia's leading and most progressive
organisations.

Diversity Dimensions

Critical neighbourhood stakeholders

The Team will facilitate a Visioning Session with each
neighborhood in their hometown. The session's
purpose is to encourage and foster collaborative efforts
among all critical neighborhood stakeholders involved
in the successful implementation and management of
the principals, strategies and recommendation's of the
Neighborhood Revitalization Action Plan.

From a request to schedule a meeting by a private firm contracted by the State of
Michigan

Sharing donorCentrics™

This presentation will share with you what donorCentrics™ is, explaining this benchmarking service that facilitates peer organisation comparison of donor lifecycle behaviour and fundraising program performance, and provides a forum for cross-organisational collaboration and the sharing of best practices in fundraising.

From an email invitation to a webcast on a new analysis service for fundraisers

Reshape your genetic code by graft

Leaders are also taught how to reshape their companies' genetic code . . . by teaching them how to graft practices into their patterns of engagement.

Benchmark Communications

Targeted solutions

We work at a strategic level to understand an organisation's human capital needs so that targeted solutions can be designed and implemented to meet business objectives.

Human Capital Management Systems

Optimal outcomes

This year's theme for Mercury World Australia is Optimize Outcomes . . . Over two exciting days we will show you how:

- Business Technology Optimization (BTO) can be applied to Optimize Outcomes . . . To leverage best practices you will learn from Mercury's experts and your peers.

Mercury World Australia

And so on ... the things they do!

We are an innovative and trusted partner who transitions, transforms and delivers world-class processes across all stages of the resourcing and recruitment lifecycle.

Alexander Mann Solutions

Achieving the optimal

To achieve optimal business availability and exceed your Service Management goals you need to:

- Take a customer-centric view of service levels

- Manage to business outcomes

- Manage services that extend across IT 'silos'

- Understand the true impact of change – planned and unplanned

- Isolate, triage and solve problems faster

From an invitation to a seminar organised by Mercury Australia

We are concerned that by now readers might be overstimulated. If you find the pounding heart and ideating mind discomforting, just think what it's like for the people who live these brands.

Ideation

Filtering. After 'ideation' ideas must be 'filtered'.

Booz Allen Hamilton

Reaching new heights of effectiveness

By working over the period of a full day with a select group of the target audience . . . we are able to cut through to the essence of required organisational imperatives to take their talent management endeavours to new heights of effectiveness.

The Stephenson Partnership Pty Ltd, which helps executives to 'free up more air-space in their diaries'

Visualising broader windows

Nuffer, Smith, Tucker is a public relations firm, founded in 1974, with expertise in the design and execution of strategies for the future, cultivating supportive stakeholder relationships and fueling the quid pro quo exchange . . . Trends intelligence systems help management and boards of directors challenge assumptions, scrutinize organization strategies and facilitate convention breaking thinking by visualizing a broader window of the future world.

Nuffer, Smith, Tucker Public Relations

Leveraging

To best address the changing needs of our diverse audience, each office is divided into core industry practices. These divisions leverage a global research base of best practices to produce an unrivalled series of conferences . . .

IQPC Australia

Executing

This process involves the following steps: strategic alignment with the vision on where to take the company, competitive differentiation, first scan attractiveness of the idea, feasibility organisational capabilities to execute cross-department inclusion, consistency of process, buy-in to output.

Report provided by consultants Booz Allan Hamilton

Driving desire

On reflection, I think I ended up driving the desire for change too quickly and became less open to advice and compassion about the impacts on individuals.

Port Phillip Council's chief executive, David Spokes, after paying a change-management consultant $600,000

Delivering (impact consistently)

We see the essence of our work as a virtuous circle of insight, impact, and trust.

We continually strive to generate deep insight into what drives value creation and competitive advantage in our clients' businesses and the economy as a whole.

We work closely with clients to convert insights into strategies, whose implementation will have a substantial positive impact on performance.

Consistently delivering impact earns the trust that is the foundation of lasting relationships. These relationships serve as a platform for still deeper insights and more significant impact.

Mission statement of Boston Consulting, a company used by the Victorian Department of Education

Developing (predictable increments intricately tied)

A facilitator tasked with developing predictable increments that are intricately tied to benchmarks, milestones, and completion dates.

James Atkins, a project manager with MediaLine, describing his position

Transitioning (to greatness)

Training Dynamics is your opportunity to transition to greatness under the guidance of a Master Trainer.

Presented in a logical yet entertaining format the techniques of Neuro Linguistic Programming and Spiral Dynamics will integrate to produce cutting edge aspects of training design and delivery.

Be able to layer and nest exercises for maximum instructional impact.

Extend your stage anchoring and platform skills.

Training Dynamics 2004

Sarah generates buzz . . .

Sarah is the celebrations architect and product manager for RedBalloon for Corporate and takes on the responsibility for generating THE BUZZ and building excitement for your corporate reward and recognition programs. Designing special program launch packs, teaser campaigns, award challenges and custom events – Sarah's dedicated to starting the conversation!

www.redballoondays.com.au

. . . by doing a fun activity on a motorbike

Objectives

St. George wanted to have their staff participate in a team building event at the conclusion of a conference, believing that it was a great way to get out their staff out of the office and do a fun activity together.

Action

Rebecca chose the Harley Davidson Motorbike Blast through Sydney. 'It was a complete surprise for my colleagues until the Harley's came cruising past and parked in front of us,' said Rebecca. The staff were able to visit all of the iconic sites of Sydney and the easy going nature of the drivers made the experience a lot of fun, plus there was the added bonus of capturing some really great photos!

Outcome

'The overall experience with RedBalloon was great. It just made things very easy for me to organize . . . The only thing that we hated was when the experience ended,' said Rebecca. St George was able to get the outcome they were looking for in terms of rewarding their staff with some much earned down time and combining it with a really fun experience.

www.redballoondays.com.au

You've had the experience of meeting: David B, Strategic Account Manager.

Business card of an employee of Red Balloon Days

Building our people

Our goal is to deliver each client tangible results, cost-effectively. We do this by building our people, our capability and our alliances to effectively leverage our key attributes and in-depth knowledge of recognition, incentive and reward practices.

Accumulate

Strengthening our thought leadership

We seek to strengthen our thought-leadership, market presence and business capability in these areas through acquisitions, alliances, expansion into new geographic markets and industry Memberships.

Accumulate

Incentivising our others

To best incentivise others you need an incentive solution that provides tangible results and incentivises the kind of behaviours that increase your business performance. The Points Shop incentive program is a flexible, customisable solution focused on bottom line business results.

www.pointsshop.com.au

Growing your people

To ensure the company continues to achieve significant benefits and your people continue to grow personally and professionally, Synergy will customise Corporate Training Programs to order. These services create an environment for both your people and your business to thrive in an ever competitive market place. Our objective is to engage your people, assist them in developing their skills and strengthen their commitment to your company.'

Synergy

Building a relevant tool

Thank you for your feedback, we do appreciate your points.

One challenge we have always faced is building a tool that is relevant to as many people as possible. One aspect that is always a factor is how people interpret certain words. Whilst this is unfortunate, it is also inevitable given the complexity of the English language.

Our hope is that the vast majority of people will interpret the word as an adjective describing a person who is concerned with people in some sort of way.

Perhaps sometimes it's easier to think of a person you would not use the word Humanistic about.

Reply to Ingrid Richardson, who had asked what Human Synergistics Australia meant by 'humanistic' in a survey it had conducted

Think of someone close to you – not Ivan the Terrible or Vlad the Impaler – you would not use the term *humanistic* about.

Compelling the adopter

Key message – Value identification drives innovation issues

I believe that a deep understanding of the 'value identification' process is critical to crafting an effective innovation policy, since it is a critical lever of innovation success rates. My reasons are set out below:

1. Value identification is an essential step

Innovation only occurs when the Value Proposition (the result of the value identification process) is compelling to the adopter (the one who has to change behaviour to implement the innovation). I believe that this is self-evident – if the Value Proposition is not compelling, the innovation won't be adopted.

Submission to National Innovation System review from David Ansley, management consultant

Excitedly cooperating

The nature of our business has enabled us to develop enduring, meaningful relationships with our clients supported by our commitment to maintaining the highest standards of quality of advice and ethics and integrity in everything we do . . . In terms of your relationship with your adviser, very little will change . . . centralising many of the functions we currently replicate, such as business administration platforms, and back office systems and procedures. Together, we are excited and enthusiastic about our ongoing cooperation and collaboration and the prospect of further jointly developed initiatives that will create benefits for our clients now, and in to the future . . . This is an exciting development in the growth of our company . . .

From an updated Financial Services Guide from Shadforths

Excellent jargon

9. Reduce jargon in all knowledge initiatives, documentation and presentation.

10. Ensure relevance of Centre of Excellence construct.

Consultant's report, Victorian Government department

Executive education

If you're going to take home two hundred times more than the average weekly wage, it might be prudent to pick up a few learnings of your own – or at least a few new phrases (which, adroitly used, are much the same thing). For little more than the cost of your second car, you can 'step into a completely new way of seeing, thinking, being and leading through executive education' (University of Melbourne, Mount Eliza). Really. You won't get that from the Dalai Lama. They're not promising an afterlife, but *strategic staircases*, *real-time interface scenarios* and *transformational journeys* are guaranteed. And you get to learn a common language.

A language all your own

We brought executives together to experience a new, shared learning and develop a common language.

Meaghan Callaghan, human resources director, SEEK

Harnessing hearts and authoritatively inspiring follower-ship

To embed your vision and values you need to ensure your Leadership Consciousness is powerful integrated and wise.

What is leadership consciousness?

It is the intangible aspect of leaders that not only establishes direction but authoritatively inspires, engages and harnesses the hearts, minds, and souls of its follower-ship.

Corporate Power

Tailored to your needs

All programs can be tailored to address your company's competencies, issues and language and can be branded with your logo.

Mount Eliza Executive Education

Moving the needle

Today, customised executive education is about 'moving the needle' for organisations in terms of business outcomes; its starts with the organisational strategy, followed by the development of people to achieve this strategy.

Mount Eliza Executive Education

Moving it in terms of

Our focus is on moving the needle for organisations in terms of business outcomes through our customised, tailored, open and coaching programs.

Mount Eliza Executive Education

Complete the following exercises (and award yourself an MBA)

Delivering value from change initiatives in today's complex and competitive environment poses significant challenges to managers. Operational improvements must be undertaken to ensure that planned business results are achieved.

Programmes and projects are normal vehicles for implementing change initiatives. Business projects primarily deliver capability building outcomes and not direct value. Programme and project management with a strong focus on project level delivery (the capability outcomes) is necessary but often insufficient to deliver the final business benefits promised in the business cases.

This 1½ day course aims to give participants a practical perspective on the concepts, approaches and techniques that can be used to facilitate the better alignment of projects with strategic goals, the integration of Benefits Management with Project Management, and a full lifecycle focus on benefits delivery, from 'concept to catch'.

Benefits Management using the Strategic Journey Mapping (SJM™) methodology is an approach to effectively plan, manage and deliver outcomes from the concept stage to achievement of benefits.

Victoria University of Wellington, New Zealand, Professional and Executive Development Course Overview

Create a PowerPoint presentation to illustrate the course overview and present it in reverse to a friend. See if she notices.

* * *

Rob and Bruce have considerable experience having developed and run strategic innovation initiatives in large organisations including a major financial services company. During the Forum they will talk to a series of actual value pools and use real life examples of strategic staircases detailing growth opportunities.

www.westernsydney.e-newsletter.com.au

Talk to an actual value pool.

* * *

SEEK sustains its entrepreneurial spirit because its leaders are able to undergo personal transformation.

www.seek.com.au

What is the connection between entrepreneurial spirit and personal transformation?

* * *

The program helped the executives achieve this through examining their leadership style and behaviours on others and in considering how these can be modified to create more powerful working relationships. It also helped them understand the links between their values and actions and their critical impact on organisational success. Executives set personal goals and action plans to embed their learnings on return to work.

Mount Eliza Executive Education

How critical is impact of the link, would you say? Think of three learnings and embed them.

* * *

Richard Barrett is the Founder and Chairman of the Barrett Values Centre. He works with CEOs and senior executives in North and South America, Europe, Australia and Asia to develop vision-guided, values-driven organisational cultures that strengthen financial performance, build cultural capital, and support sustainable development. He is the creator of the internationally recognised Cultural Transformation Tools (CTT) which have been used to support more than 1000 organisations in 42 countries in their transformational journeys.

www.valuescentre.com

Create your own CTT and take a transformational journey. Are there any other kinds of journeys it can take you on?

* * *

Self-efficacy is the perception/belief people have about their capacity to achieve in relation to actions and goals.

www.iecoaching.com

Explain in a haiku.

* * *

Coaching is a collaborative relationship that uses an adult learning framework to help the coachee identify and remove any interference that limits the expression of their full potential. Performance is improved through an integral view of what interferes with potential. The coaching relationship is framed within an adult learning cycle that encourages a systematic, solution-focused process of:

- setting goals,

- taking actions that ensure sustainable behaviour change, and

- reflecting to make sense of these changes in terms of new understandings, initial individual goals, desired organisational results and long-term, personal potential.

www.iecoaching.com

Commit to memory.

* * *

Our wargame specialists design games to reveal operational synergies, accommodate a wide range of scenarios, and explore the role of the latest technologies. Our state-of-the-art wargaming and modeling facilities give senior defense and business executives the ability to test advanced concepts, conduct integrated training, and engage in real-time interactive scenarios, including distributed simulations.

Booz Allen Hamilton consultants

Engage in a real-time interactive scenario of your own and distribute the simulations.

* * *

With his help I'm now focusing on my strengths,
maximising my achievement thinking and
making subtle changes that make a big difference day
to day.

Eric Napper, Executive Producer, Australian Broadcasting Corporation

Make some subtle changes to yourself.

* * *

The coaching helped me to reflect on my strengths
and weaknesses, and to be able to articulate clearly the
value-add I could bring to an organisation, as well as
my key achievements. So often we take for granted what
we do everyday, and don't see it as a skill or a strength
— when quite often it really is!

www.pacificconsulting.com.au

What value-add do you think you have ever brought to
anything?

* * *

I can't even begin to tell you how empowered I am now
after our coaching. I'm spending two-thirds of my
week building relationships.

Professor Jeanette Ward, former area director, NSW Health

What is Professor Ward actually doing?

Strategy

You need a strategy. You need to be strategic. Even if you don't know what it is, or what it means, or how to spell it – you still need it. You need a strategy to *achieve outcomes*, of which the first is *achieving strategy*. Without a strategy you can't have *goals*, or even *values*, much less a *road map*, and without these you will never achieve significant *alignment*, and your *vision* will remain unachieved: a horrible fate indeed. What's almost as bad, you'll never be able to write or utter a sentence, not in any advanced place of work, at least. Once you have a strategy, pretty well everything exists *in terms of* it.

Some people confuse their *strategy* with their *plan*. This is wrong. They're different, as any fool can tell just by looking at the words. Take, 'We will leave no stone unturned in terms of making sure that we get back into a winning vein.' Turning over stones is not a strategy in terms of anything – unless you expect to find your vision under one of them. As a rule of thumb, a plan achieves your goal and a strategy achieves your vision.

Sometimes the goal of your plan is achieving your strategy, which means achieving your vision is also the goal of your plan. The same goes for *tactics*; as one blog wisely notes, 'Collecting low-hanging fruit is a knowledge management tactic NOT a legitimate strategy.' But try not to let it get this complicated.

In terms of Telstra

SOL TRUJILLO: So you've gotten a view about our strategy, you've got a view from Greg about what we've been doing as an integrated company building this, and then you've heard from John in terms of where we're at, in terms of our plans financially, the view going forward in terms of costs takeout . . .

Telstra Investor Day, November 2008

In terms of dongles

RICHARD EARY: First going on to Next G, in terms of the road map, in terms of devices, obviously I think the launch of the dongles on megs, and early next year, can you just give a feel in terms of what the road map is going to be actually for physical handsets? So far as I'm aware, we're still quite a way from actually getting megabyte handsets in the market in terms of mass scale.

Telstra Investor Day, November 2008

In terms of procurement, going forward

RICHARD EARY: I mean clearly with the way the Aussie dollar has moved, I don't know whether you can give us a better feel in terms of how that implements or affects the transformation plans over the next couple of years in terms of procurement from suppliers, obviously Bright Star, some of the contracts have been hedged going forward, but outside of that, but also from the equipment side, a lot of the actual purchases are done locally in Aussie dollar contracts . . .

Telstra Investor Day, November 2008

Love for children strategy

We look forward to working in partnership with you to provide high quality child care solutions as part of an innovative and retention strategy . . . Our love for children also lives outside our centres.

ABC Learning Centres

A strategy for brilliant success

These strategic themes will enable Synergy to realise its vision:

By 2009 we will transform Synergy into a brilliantly successful retailer. The skills, experience and passion of our people will make Synergy the brand of choice in a highly competitive energy market . . . We will make a difference in our community by delivering on our environmental and social commitments.

Synergy

Organic strategy

Importantly we are fortunate to have a talented and experienced executive team at St George that will continue to execute our organic strategy.

John Thame, chairman of St George Bank

Vegetable strategy (inorganic)

The implementation plan provides detailed strategies to improve opportunities for the Tasmanian Vegetable Industry. To ensure implementation of the strategy, and at the request of the Tasmanian

Farmers and Graziers Association, I have appointed a new implementation committee. It will drive the implementation of the proposed strategies.

David Llewellyn, Tasmanian Primary Industries Minister

New growth strategy

This headline result was in line with expectations as we transition the business through its transformation program and commence implementation of the new growth strategy.

Letter to shareholders from Rick Allert, chairman of the Coles Group

Achieving strategy

(Company name) provides operator based services to streamline operational procedure with the intent of achieving strategic effect through the efficient use of tactical applications.

A private-sector brochure promoting a seminar for members of the Australian intelligence community

Conspicuous strategies

These IEPs are structured using conspicuous strategies and mediated scaffolding to ensure learning strategies are developed, understood and retained, as well as the achievement of the learning outcomes.

Teachers' application for promotions

Strategic staircase

Course contents – Strategy for internal consultants . . .

- causal mapping
- drivers and KPIs
- the strategic staircase

- strategic implementation
- culture and leadership
- the Balanced Scorecard

www.internal-consulting.co.uk/strategy.php

Building front-end strategy

I'm responsible for direct strategy and building front end and lead generation for all business channels, which incorporate advisory, business finance and debtor finance.

The CEO of *The Australian Financial Review*

Feedback on the operational of the realigned model strategy

XX and XXX would now like to present that feedback to the team in the form of a workshop where we step through various scenarios using the revised accountability workflow; and also discuss how we will be implementing and collecting additional feedback on the operational of the realigned model over the next 3 months – process champions, collection of future feedback, current actions outstanding, etc. This workshop represents the gateway for operational use of the workflows . . . Please make the time to attend this last-off meeting so we can roll straight into the strategic work with the engagement guidelines in place and being monitored from this point.

From an email. Subject: Project Wrap-Up – Cross-team process review and alignment

A long-term strategy

Proactively influences and participates in strategic decision-making on issues when engaging with senior managers and staff to establish long term strategies to determine the future direction for the organisation and their area of accountability.

Resume

Communication strategy

Members of the Project Steering Committee of the Confidence Building Stakeholder Involvement-Nile Basin Initiative . . . discussed in detail issues including the Mid-Year January-June 2008 Progress Report to the challenges involved in setting up the Institutional Strengthening Project (ISP) and the urgent need in finalizing the CBSI Communication Strategy.

Nile Basin Initiative, Shared Vision Program

Strategy taken forward (with sympathy for the potential outcome)

I know it's an emotive issue . . . but we can't apologise for taking the strategy forward in the way we have, and the outcomes we have achieved. While we have some sympathy for the potential outcome we've got to be looking at the bigger picture all the time.

Federal Police Commissioner Mick Keelty, talking about sharing intelligence with Indonesian police

Management strategy

Whilst no formal terms of reference exist for the MIG, the CCG agreed in principle that the functions of the MIG should be to . . . liaise with the State Crisis Centre (if activated) to ensure effective integration of a crisis and consequence management strategies.

Department of Emergency Services, Queensland

Swimming strategy

The objective of the review is to assist Swimming New Zealand examine and creatively challenge themselves to arrive at a collectively owned vision for the sport and a framework ensuring their successful operation and growth to 2008 and beyond . . . Through the review it is expected also that areas of best practice and areas for possible enhancement will be identified to support the implementation and successful achievement of current and future strategies, in essence providing a 'Blueprint' for the future of swimming in New Zealand.

'A Blue Print for the Future', Revitalisation Report, Swimming New Zealand, July 2004

Strategy upon strategy

This strategic framework for the information economy sets out a vision for the information economy for 2004 to 2006, four broad objectives, four strategic priorities and 16 supporting strategies for the information economy.

'Australia's Strategic Framework for the Information Economy 2004–2006 – Opportunities and Challenges for the Information Age', Federal government policy document

Rather like a *mission*, or a *vision*, or a *buy-in* or an *uptake*, once you have a *strategy*, it's wonderful to see how everyone uses the same words.

Compelling retail visitations strategy

Successful execution of the Melbourne Retail Strategy 2006–2012 will ultimately increase visitation and spend to Melbourne's retail core and further develop Melbourne's unique retail offer.

John So, Lord Mayor of Melbourne

In 2012 Melbourne will be renowned globally as
Australia's leading retail city with an unrivalled retail
landscape acclaimed for its diversity and compelling
experiences.

Melbourne Retail Strategy mission statement

This retail strategy is the first of its kind and will
provide a focused plan to ensure that by 2012
Melbourne will be renowned globally as Australia's
leading retail city with an unrivalled retail
landscape acclaimed for its diversity and compelling
experiences.

Andre Haermeyer, Victorian Minister for Manufacturing and Export, Financial
Services and Small Business

Staircase strategy

5.3: Officers are currently aligning the budget setting
and business planning process and a revised approach
to Star Chamber and service planning is being
introduced and is covered elsewhere on the agenda.
This will include a corporate balance scorecard and
strategic staircase at corporate and strategic levels.

Slough Borough Council

Lobbying strategy (revised) to process overall impact

5.12: Currently analysis is being undertaken to
determine the overall impact for Slough in relation
to the rest of the Country. On the face of the figures
Slough appears to be gaining at a faster rate and if the
detailed analysis confirms this, then a revised lobbying
strategy will be drawn together to process this . . .

Slough Borough Council

Key strategies

The ultimate test of Centrelink's performance is the achievement of key strategies for each of our goals.

Centrelink

Synergistic strategy

Our decision to form strategic partnerships with other progressive companies is synergistic with ImageSource's business strategy to be a leader in the facility management, print and imaging industry.

Image Source

Innovative and retention strategy

We look forward to working in partnership with you to provide high quality child care solutions as part of an innovative and retention strategy.

ABC Learning Centres Corporate Care

Madoff's multiple stock baskets strategy

Madoff's strategy is designed around multiple stock baskets made up of 30–35 stocks most correlated to the S&P 100 index. In marketing material issued by Fairfield Sentry, the sale of the calls is described as increasing 'the standstill rate of return, while allowing upward movement of the stock portfolio to the strike price of the calls'. The puts, according to the same material, are 'funded in large part by the sale of the calls, [and] limit the portfolio's downside.

'A bullish or bearish bias can be achieved by adjusting the strike prices of the options, overweighting the puts, or underweighting the calls.

However, the underlying value of the S&P 100 puts is always approximately equal to that of the portfolio of stocks,' the marketing document concludes.

MAR/Hedge (RIP) No. 89, May 2001

A plan to portray a vision (of fewer dead children)

In devising the plan members of the LSCB were mindful about the need to ensure the basic building blocks of a sound child protection system were in place. You will see from the business plan that we have created a vision statement, which is about improvement.

In light of this recent work on the business plan and our focus on practice in creating the plan, the meeting of the 22nd looked at whether we needed to amend the plan and concentrated on how the plan could be operationalised, to ensure we do the simple things well and thus safeguard the children of Conwy and Denbighshire.

The strategic plan is an important milestone in the development of the joint Denbighshire and Conwy Local Safeguarding Board. It is the result of a series of events aimed at enabling a wide range of contribution and aims to portray the long-term vision . . .

The resulting vision is that by 2012, the board will have:

Improved the protection and safeguarding of children and young people in Denbighshire and Conwy, and in particular children and young people who have experienced problems linked with:

- Mental health
- Domestic abuse
- Substance misuse . . .

Which will be achieved by:

- Improving the corporate and strategic awareness around safeguarding children and young people . . .

- Ensuring core business delivery by getting 'the simple things right' . . .

Denbighshire and Conwy Local Safeguarding Children Board Strategic Plan 2008–2012, a local government response after responsible authorities failed to prevent the brutal death of Baby 'P' in north London

Events

In a *birth event* we come into the world and in a *death event* we leave. In between, we live through many *life events*, including very often, *marriage events, divorce events, rain, hail* and *shine events, fire and flood* (or '*overbank*') *events, coronary* and other *adverse health events*. It comes back to the great existential question – why do events happen? How do we know? Is it enough to say, 'I think I am an event, therefore I am'?

Birth event

Midwives must notify the Department of Health of the outcomes of all birth events (cases) attended, regardless of the outcome . . .

WA Department of Health

Life event

Centrelink will also work to deepen its life events model including looking at where it can add value for customers by connecting them to new services.

Centrelink Future Directions 2004–2009

Marriage enrichment event

Laity need to experience a model of marriage enrichment events so they can see what's needed and what they are being asked to do — useful to advertise for support couples amongst couples at an event, as they have already experienced it for themselves. Potential support couples could be given subsidised places, or a simple job that suits their skills, such as managing the background music, or serving drinks, so that they can taste an event.

www.churchesandfamilies.org

Child event

Entitlement to the tax offset is dealt with in proposed section 61-355 which provides that a person will be entitled to the offset if:

- the person had a child event in relation to a child . . .
- the person did not have a child event in respect of another child and at that time also satisfied the following conditions . . .

Australian Taxation Laws Amendment (Baby Bonus) Bill 2002

Major type fire event

The conditions are right for a fairly major type fire event.

CFA duty officer Gregg Paterson

Adverse medicine event

Reducing the incidence of adverse medicine events (AMEs) has been difficult as there was no official channel for Australian consumers to document such events.

Australian Commission on Safety and Quality in Health Care

Rain event

The latest rain event has brought a mixed response from farmers across the state.

www.abc.net.au/rural

Mixed rain event

Yes, I realize that this is probably going to be a mixed or mix-to-rain event, but still, this is a nice image!

www.voices.washingtonpost.com

Extreme precipitation event

Edmonton Extreme Precipitation Event July 11, 2004. In the afternoon of July 11 2004 southern sections of Edmonton City were struck by a small scale but extreme rain and hail event in association with a cold low.

SkyscraperPage Forum

Snow event

This is a big snow event. Although it's going to be exciting for some, it could really cause some major disruption . . . We are in for a significant, disruptive snowfall event.

The Met Office has previously used the terms 'organised rain'.

www.dailymail.co.uk

Volcano event

I've actually been trying to find a way of including the Chaiten Volcano event in the Universe Today for the last few days, but apart from doing a minor story of an International Space Station snapshot from orbit, I couldn't find much bulk for the report.

Ian O'Neill, Astroengine.com

Extreme climactic event

Just on your warning yesterday that we can expect more of these extreme climactic events, and you've repeated today at the Summit; how is that going to be factored into planning for these events in the future?

A reporter questions John Brumby, Premier of Victoria

Wind event

Well, I think that's exactly why we're holding an event like today . . . when I met with the insurance industry a couple of months ago and, for them, they said, you know, the biggest issue, risk issue — they're in the risk management business — and the biggest issue for them going forward is how they manage wind events, because for every ten kilometres an hour you get up over 50 or 60 or 70 kilometres an hour, the damage doubles . . .

John Brumby, Premier of Victoria

Wind event (2)

'It's not so much a heat event today, it's a wind event and you are going to see intense winds,' he [Brumby] told 3AW radio.

John Brumby, Premier of Victoria

Wind event (3)

·'There is an expectation that under the wind event on Tuesday that fire will break out and make a run towards Melbourne water catchments,' Mr Brown said.

'Minister warns of fire danger ahead', *The Age*, 1 March 2009

Very big wind event

'It's a very, very big wind event that we're looking at over the Tuesday period and in fact into Wednesday,' the bureau's Mark Williams said . . .

'"We're not crying wolf": fires, high winds to hit state tonight', *The Age*, 2 March 2009

Unbelievable wind event

What happened with the wind event is that a lot of the lines between the street and the house came down, so you've got literally hundreds – in fact, I understand there may be thousands – where that single line coming in from the power pole has been broken . . . very, very unusual . . . The issue is we just had this unbelievable wind event off the back of what was a subtropical cyclone . . .

www.premier.vic.gov.au

Storm event

You are going to see that wind come up today, this is a storm event and it will be very similar to April last year.

Herald Sun, 3 March 2009

Thunderstorm event

'In Adelaide, more thunderstorms were recorded than normal,' he said. 'In fact we had four events of thunderstorms compared to our normal one event in January.'

Bureau of Meteorology spokesperson

Unforeseen event

The incident was caused by an unforeseen geological event.

A construction company responsible for building the Lane Cove Tunnel (Sydney) apologising for the partial collapse of a section of the project – under a block of flats

Non-ongoing event

The reason we're doing this is to enable us to have time to try to source where this cryptosporidium came from to ensure that this is an event, rather than something which might be ongoing.

Phil Koperberg, Water Minister of New South Wales, following the detection of low levels of a diarrhoea-causing parasite in Sydney's catchment

'Significant life event, where is thy sting?'

Recognising significant life events.

Slogan of the Registry of Births, Deaths and Marriages, Victoria

Going forward

What's the alternative? Going round in circles? Going sideways? Reverse? Nothing else makes sense. That's why we say it – to affirm the direction we want to go. It comes naturally with *buy-in*. How people made progress before this is a great mystery. They had no strategy, no goals; in terms of alignment, zilch. No alignment = no going forward. Just stumbling around in the fog of history.

Some people prefer *moving forward* to *going forward*, or they combine them – even in the same sentence. This is acceptable usage: it is the direction that counts, and the sense of swirling, unstoppable progress. Like a mighty river, or Sol Trujillo.

Going forward in terms of the back parts of an architecture

Let me say it again: we have architected our business for a high speed broadband world . . . This is not old Telstra any more, it is the new Telstra, highly competitive, highly focussed and very results-driven in terms of what we do . . . You're going to see us continue to leverage the existing assets that we have . . . we will let you know if anything changes in terms of how we think about our company going forward . . .

So you've gotten a view about our strategy, you've got a view from Greg about what we've been doing as an integrated company building this, and then you've heard from John in terms of where we're at, in terms of our plans financially, the view going forward in terms of costs takeout . . . You saw the value of an architecture of a strategy that's associated with the front-end, the back-end, and the middle parts of the business.

Sol Trujillo, Telstra Investor Day, 6 November 2008

Well, look, obviously I think there is — and I don't want to presuppose anything going forward because, again, to build on the original question, we're asking for a plan over the course of the next 60 days that we think meets the test of viability . . . I think you heard him talk today about ensuring — ensuring warranties, ensuring through additional staffing that people will be in auto communities and talking to workers about ensuring that they have the benefits that they need and that the communities that support these auto industries get what they need going forward . . . Obviously there's some degree of — as the President talked about, Chrysler needing — needing partners going forward . . . President gets into the communities and talks directly to workers that would be impacted by any event, either going forward or that has already resulted in cutbacks or unemployment.

Press briefing by White House press secretary Robert Gibbs, 30 March 2009

But I think we need to see further policy going forward including future rate cuts and the fiscal stimulus.

Shane Oliver, AMP Capital Investors

We believe it is prudent to take all appropriate measures to conserve existing capital while weighing our options going forward.

Jack Armstrong, president and CEO of Genaera

The most important thing to do is to make sure that we have a plan for going forward.

Citigroup Chief Executive, Vikram Pandit

. . . they were all sold by the end of the financial year, going forward.

Rural Focus, Radio West

Processes and documentation are being development to expedite the evaluation and prioritisation of enhancements going forward.

Memo to staff from General Manager Customer Services – Country Energy

But there's always room for further continuous improvement, going forward. . .

John Brumby, Premier of Victoria

Well, it was a clear commitment in '99. It was suggested as a very good idea at the time and, because it was an election commitment, we implemented it, but at the end of the day, the market is the test in these things and, you know, the market has not supported it in a way which is viable, going forward.

John Brumby, Premier of Victoria

It was to get Toyota across the line on this announcement and to make sure that what might have been a question mark going forward becomes an affirmative decision.

John Brumby, Premier of Victoria

. . . add nuts and bolts on the options that people can embrace going forwards.

'Rural Focus', Radio West

We've also continued to make steps to improve the disclosure and stakeholder engagement regimes. And most importantly for me, we've filled most key roles and the new leadership team is shaping the business going forward.

Gordon Davis, Australian Wheat Board CEO, ABC 'World Today'

SBS believes that, going forward, a more substantial and sustained campaign is needed. ([Furthermore . . .] A key element will be to coordinate campaigns across stakeholder groups to have maximum impact on consumers. As outlined later in this submission, SBS considers that the overarching campaign should eventually be coordinated through a switchover implementation body.')

Submission to the Department of Communications, Information Technology and the Arts

Due to the representative nature of the Implementation Joint Steering Committee it should have a lead role in managing communications within local government going forward.

Water and Sewerage Reform State and Local Government Joint Implementation Steering Committee, Meeting No I, Agenda Item 5. Tasmanian Government Tenders

The truth about Labor's industrial relations system is it's all about going forward.

Julia Gillard, Deputy Prime Minister of Australia

It is also an opportunity for me to welcome very much the fact that we now have the Australian convict sites nomination going forward.

Peter Garrett, federal member for Kingsford Smith

He was really good and hopefully going forward that can really help the team, and for us to play some key forwards around Pav to help him out when he is there.

Freemantle Dockers' coach, Mark Harvey

What are your predictions going forward for where markets should head in the next quarter, and what are the key factors you see coming up in the next quarter?

www.forbes.com

I learnt a lot and I'm still trying to carry on that information of what she was able to give me there with every match going forward.

Samantha Stosur, tennis player

. . . it is a platform for going forward again with our bilateral arrangements . . . In fact, trade is very much a solution to stronger economic growth going forward because trade is a multiplier . . .

Simon Crean, on ABC Radio, 27 February 2009

We don't see anything as a risk going forward, but as an opportunity,

Eddie Groves, Chief Executive, ABC Child Care Centres, 19 Feb 2007

Please cc Promotions Group on a go forward. Thx, Laura

An email submitted to www.weaselwords.com.au

5. I have a clear sense of how to improve my performance going forward.

From an employee opinion survey

ALI MOORE: On the basis of your own assessment, it seems a very fundamental and comprehensive repudiation of previous strategy. Would shareholders be justified in asking what they've been paying management and the board for over recent years?

IAN JOHNSON (CEO of Foster's): . . . And I wouldn't necessarily say that this is a repudiation; it is actually us learning from mistakes and moving forward . . . I would just say, some of this is natural succession and some of it is upgrading our capability. And I do think we have the chance to move forward into a whole new era . . . What I am there to do is to analyse what we can do going forward, what's sensible for us as a business . . . I think that new management and a number of new directors would give you confidence this is not the same people saying the same things from the past. And we have the benefit of a very exhaustive review which is now, I think, the platform for us to move forward . . .

And I think that we – with our strong financial position, we should be able to continue to deliver returns on this business which are better than our peer group at which, pretty well they have been, and which continue to deliver yield for the shareholders and upside potential for them, as they go forward . . .

ALI MOORE: I've never spoken to a CEO who hasn't espoused all those very same values . . .

Lateline, ABC TV, 17 February 2009

This is a global problem . . . but we have a plan going forward.

Kevin Rudd, Prime Minister of Australia

Synergy

Synergy is the energy you get from putting complementary things – or elements of a thing – together. Think Tracy and Hepburn; Brad and Angelina; music and dance; sausages and mustard; starlight and teardrops. Then think of one without the other. Life is impossible without synergy and, being so much a part of life, managers need it too. The word is Greek and means *work together* – which means, when you think about the world, it's pretty well everywhere.

The thing is to find it. Synergy is as real as the feeling you get from eating a good pineapple, and just as invisible. It takes an expert to find it; and as if to prove the synergies of the marketplace, consultants have evolved to fill the need. There are hordes of them, many with the word *synergy* in their name. They'll come to your place, run their divining rods over the premises and find the hidden synergies within. Soon your corporate chakras will be humming and you'll be intoning 'synergy' and synergy-related words like a veritable swami. Call a synergy consultant now; and if they can't come straight away, get on to a Feng Shui whiz until they can.

Aspects of synergies

The positive energies and outcomes evident in Marion seem to be a product of fertile connections between groups eager to learn, explore new models and use technology to further their ends. Some aspects of the Marion synergies such as the Seniors-On-Line and the South Ward Neighbourhood Network have been long established. Other dimensions, such as the Learning Festival and Cultural Centre, are newer and the possible additional synergies are unpredictable.

www.marion.sa.gov.au

Significant cost synergy opportunities

The outcome of our analysis is that this transaction meets our shareholder return hurdles, and our M&A disciplines. It is strongly NPV positive and EPS accretive within 3 years, and importantly it's strongly accretive in the following years. We are focused on four areas of synergy and growth opportunity.

Secondly there remains significant cost synergy opportunities, notwithstanding the retention of both branch and other distribution networks . . .

Conference call regarding St George/Westpac merger May 2008, www.westpac.com.au/manage/pdf

Exploring synergies

An executable strategy for leveraging transferable skills and exploring cross team synergies will result in higher competency and resource utilisation in an organisation.

'Leveraging cross team synergies', Sunder Ramachandran and Madan Ramachandran, www.ascent.com

Getting a handle on synergies

Hi Gail, hi Phil. I just want to get a better handle on the synergy topic and also ACCC concern, but I guess with synergies just a better feel for year 2 . . .

Conference call, www.westpac.com.au/manage/pdf

Playing through the synergies

Jeff it's Phil, with regard to the synergies, the timing of when this becomes earnings per share [EPS] accretive is obviously a function of the timing at which the costs of integration play through and the timing at which the cost synergies play through and we have specified that it becomes EPS accretive in the 3rd year because that allows us to, I think, indicate in a conservative way how we think the timing of those 2 large elements will play through . . .

Conference call, www.westpac.com.au/manage/pdf

Parking synergy

Everyone's working to build a synergy downtown, and we're going to need more parking.

Jeff Weninger, Chandler City Council, Arizona Central

In synergy with instruments

Held under Chatham House rules to allow for a candid and constructive discussion the discussion focused on governments' roles in the effort to fight corruption and how the OECD Guidelines can be used in synergy with other anti-corruption instruments.

Foreign Investment Review Board Annual Report, www.firb.gov.au

Achieving synergies

Whilst we are very positive about our revenue opportunities, we also haven't in our modelling, looked to be overly optimistic in our revenue synergies because we also know that they are more difficult to be prescriptive about and the market obviously looks to provide a higher probability on cost [synergies being achieved].

Conference call, www.westpac.com.au/manage/pdf

Synergy in the tank

On the eve of the 2007 World Cup, the world cricketing community is left wondering whether, with the retirement of Martyn, McGrath already having handed in his notice, and Symonds and Lee incapacitated, Ponting's side has enough synergy left in its tank to retain its hold on one of cricket's most coveted trophies.

Sportstar Weekly, 17 March 2007

Obvious synergy

The report on innovation makes some pertinent points about the synergies between competition policy in the 1990's and its transition to a macroeconomic instrument as this relates to IP in the new millennium . . .

There are obvious synergy between IP policy implementation, driven at a regulatory level, and wider macroeconomic policy, including competition policy.

DFAT briefing on the current state of ACTA

Hair synergy

The ultimate objective of Hair Synergy is to restore hair to people with balding and hair loss problems. The parallel objective is to educate and create awareness to the public concerning the latest, state-of-the-art options for hair loss treatment that are available, as well as dispelling some common myths of hair transplantation.

Hair Synergy and Care, sg.88db.com

Synergy crisis

What's the synergy crisis? It is a soundbite for a complex, long-term problem involving bureaucratic turf battles and lack of focused leadership that costs America lives, time and money. America has trouble synchronizing its 'tools of national power' — synergizing its diplomatic, information, military and economic power to achieve a policy goal, like winning a war.

www.strategypage.com

Branding

Who am I? Why do I exist? *Do* I exist? How do I differ from a Christmas beetle or a filing cabinet? Can it be that I am just another blob of the same banal ectoplasm of which the jerk at the next desk to me is made? Of course, you can look to God for solutions to these questions, but in business branding has all the answers you need. Your *mission* and *vision statements* will

give you more self-definition, for sure. Your *values* will put meat on the bone. *Buy-in* will make you whole. But who cares, if no one else knows? Without a brand you may as well be extinct.

A country

Our brand is our people. Australians are loved around the world because we don't take ourselves too seriously.

Designer Hans Hulsbosch, *Sun-Herald*, May 2009

A city

This is huge for them, huge for the name brand of Geelong . . .

Victorian Premier John Brumby, on Geelong winning the AFL Grand Final in 2007

It's not good for us, but it keeps the New Orleans brand out there.

New Orleans Mayor Ray Nagin's take on murders in his city

A university

As part of the branding strategy for the University . . . we now have a new process for the development of creative concepts for advertising purposes . . . all creative work will be referred to the agency appointed to help develop the University's brand identity . . . This is to ensure that we consistently deliver 'on brand' communication . . . we are aiming to be the 'challenger' brand in the education market. The brand personality is a key tool for differentiating Victoria University. It has been defined as:

- can do, expressive, cheeky, brave
- open minded, suprising

- straight talking, individual: and

- worldly, friendly.

From a highly confidential document: 'Developing "street smart" creative', outlining Victoria University's new approach to marketing

A health care service

In 2008, Mercy Health & Aged Care underwent a rebranding. As a consquence of this process, the following facility names have changed . . .

www.mercy.com.au

An island

The Brand Tasmania Council's vision is that Tasmania be recognised as a leader in the world of islands, with a global reputation for quality products and services.

Brand Tasmania

A mosque

Alpha Data has been selected by the General Authority of Islamic Affairs to install a centralised digital signage system in mosques throughout the UAE. Worshippers will be able to view information on all aspects of religion mixed with specific day-to-day activities relating to their local mosques . . . Centrally controlled digital signage offers a mechanism by which 'head office' can continue to drive standards — and by distributing high quality messaging, ensure that the right 'brand ideals' are getting through.

www.ameinfo.com

A church

The Fellowship's identity-altering situation reflects an ongoing trend that sees American congregations becoming ever conscious and purposeful in selecting and marketing their names, said Mara Einstein, an expert on church marketing and branding and a media studies professor at Queens College in New York.

www.jacksonville.com

A hockey team

We aim to maximise the impact and the value of our identity by presenting a professional and consistent public face that is strongly 'hockey' . . . It is mandatory that we remain consistent and remain true to the values of the Hockey WA brand . . . No deviation from these guidelines by way of adaptation or alteration is acceptable . . . Ultimately, the consumer will establish a pattern of instant recognition . . .

Hockey WA Branding Guidelines

An industry

The APIC 2008 conference was amazing with incredible presentations addressing all of the hot-topics for infection prevention. Yes, you read correctly — in Denver APIC took the bold step of re-branding our profession. This rebranding included a new title for our work. From Denver onwards we will be known as INFECTION PREVENTIONISTS. It's a mouthful but promises to elevate the profession in public, professional and governmental arenas all around the world.

A Day In The Life Of An APIC Board Member blog

A mercenary army

The company [Blackwater] has been reorganizing for several months to 'create unique brand identities for its products and services'.

The (Norfolk) *Virginian-Pilot*

A suitcase

SmartPack has developed an exciting range of marketing initiatives to drive the brand forward, with a vision to be the preferred luggage brand for the world's smart travellers.

From the SmartPack website, www.smartpack.biz

An internal brand

The useful concept of internal branding has been around in the UK and US for about 12 or 13 years, and there have been more than a dozen articles on the subject in *Strategic Communication Management* . . . Yet here in Australia there is still a lot of confusion. I even heard a communication 'heavy' introduce a session recently using the terms internal branding and employer branding interchangeably. Others simply think that all you need to do to deliver the brand promise is to fire-up employees, totally ignoring the impact of product quality, systems and processes. This presentation explains what internal branding is and the role of internal communication in helping to deliver the brand promise.

www.employee-communication.com.au

We understood nothing until we understood branding. Adam Smith, Darwin, Marx, Freud – none of them understood that in every little thing there sleeps a brand. Nothing exists that cannot be branded, provided you employ the right branding consultant.

Branding fee for revenue uplift

Customers Ltd will lose the convenience fee that Bendigo and Adelaide customers would otherwise have paid to use the machines but will pick up what the announcement refers to as a 'branding fee' and which, according to the announcement, will generate 'revenue uplift' for the firm . . . The deployment of branded ATM networks and arrangements with other networks of branded ATMs (but confusingly known as sub-networks in the industry jargon) may be becoming a point of difference for banks and independent ATM owners.

www.thesheet.com

We build brands that drive revenue

At The Blake Project we design, manage and build brands that drive revenue through differentiated customer experiences.

That could mean delivering one or more of the following: brand audits, brand research, brand strategy, brand (re)positioning, brand architecture, brand identity, brand management, brand measurement, brand marketing, brand extension, brand education, internal brand building, brand building on the Internet/social media, 'out-of-the-box' marketing, sensory branding and international speaking engagements with an emphasis on branding. We also help with customer touchpoint design.

www.theblakeproject.com

Ms Monaghan's rebranding experience

As Marketing Manager, Ms Monaghan's role encompasses brand recognition, corporate marketing, group-wide communication, and business development. She has extensive experience in rebranding acquisitions.

www.gallipoliresearch.com.au

Branded employer of first choice

By combining our expertise in values research, market planning, marketing communications and human capital, we have developed a remarkable understanding of employer branding, including what it takes to be viewed as an employer of first choice.

www.research.com.au

The most latent and subconscious desires revealed

With Brad VanAuken, we have developed a number of qualitative and quantitative research approaches to identify the most latent customer hopes, fears, anxieties, desires and other subconscious motivations that can be used in brand positioning.

The Blake Project

Brands with emotional benefits

A person's perception of a brand is the result of all the interactions he or she has had with the brand, including the product or service itself, the purchase and usage experiences, what others are saying about the brand, and what the person sees, hears or reads about the brand. The brand might deliver any combination of functional, emotional, experiential or self-expressive benefits. And the brand essence, promise and personality must be consistently and compellingly manifested at each point of contact the brand makes with the customer. Finally, the brand's position can be reinforced through any of the senses.

The Blake Project

Brand management is supposed to go beyond the literal and functional to strike at emotions. As a brand, the [CIA] site does connote some emotions, such as excessive amount of data and lack of coordination, which is probably not the sought-after positioning strategy.

www.brandchannel.com

Be vigilant about your brand (and act upon input)

Personally this is a very exciting time. A time of great opportunity and one which I am sure APIC will guide with great vision. As this change is implemented I am sure that the Board and the APIC staff will constantly be vigilant and in touch with the membership as their views are sought and their input acted upon.

A Day In The Life Of An APIC Board Member blog

You will like Tasmania, or else

The Brand Tasmania Council is committed to the promotion and protection of the Tasmanian Brand and the values that constitute that brand in national and international markets . . . In order to join the Brand Tasmania organisations must demonstrate a commitment to the Tasmanian brand values and agree to meet the membership criteria.

Brand Tasmania

Thou shalt have no other hockey shirt before me

These guidelines are your tool for the correct use of Hockey WA logo, Mission Statement, Vision Statement and footer in a range of applications. They contain the design controls and examples of their application which will both inspire and help you to achieve the required level of consistency . . .

- Hockey WA logo must remain separate on all sides from text and other graphic elements by a space equal to its height.

- The stick and ball in the logo cannot be used separately

- Hockey WA will not be shortened to HWA

- Hockey WA will always have a space between 'Hockey' and 'WA'

Nor make unto thee any graven image

- The mandatory font to use with Hockey WA logo is ArialMT for graphics, programmes and promotional material.

- If creating documents specifically for children the font to be used is Kristen Optional.

Nor take thy hockey name in vain

Verbal use of the logos

- When referring to Hockey WA no reference will ever be made to 'The Association', 'WAHA', 'WAWHA' or 'The Stadium'.

- Never use Hockey Western Australia

- 'We want HOCKEY EVERYWHERE' should be included in speeches and loudspeaker announcements where appropriate and as often as possible.

Hockey WA

University brand

[A design agency developed a 'brand architecture' for Monash University, because the previous logo:]

- could not deliver the brand architecture;

- did not deliver the desired positioning; and

- was not seen as a logo that is immediately linked to a high quality education provider.

[The benefits of the new logo are:] flexibility and clarity in communicating key components of Monash University, reinforcing Monash University as a high quality, innovative and international teaching and research institution.

Monash University

What happens if you discover that you're not who you think you are?

. . . As part of its rebranding, the company is jettisoning the name Blackwater and its red-and-black bear-claw logo.

www.upi.com

Blackwater Worldwide is abandoning its tarnished brand name as it tries to shake a reputation battered by oft-criticised work in Iraq, renaming its family of two dozen businesses under the name Xe. The parent company's new name is pronounced like the letter z . . . The decision comes as part of an ongoing rebranding effort that grew more urgent following a September 2007 shooting in Iraq that left at least a dozen civilians dead. Blackwater president Gary

Jackson said in a memo to employees the new name reflects the change in company focus away from the business of providing private security.

Associated Press, 13 February 2009

Blackwater has 'created, fostered and refused to curb a culture of lawlessness and unaccountability' among its employees, said Washington lawyer Susan L. Burke, lead attorney for Wijdan Mohsin Saed, 32, and her two sons, Sajjad Raheem Khalaf, 11, and Ali Raheem Khalaf, 8 . . . Beyond the specific incident, the lawsuit alleges that Blackwater never disciplined or fired guards who killed innocent Iraqis and that heavily armed Blackwater employees were routinely sent into Baghdad while under the influence of steroids and other 'judgment-altering substances.'

Los Angeles Times, 21 March 2009

Drivers and key drivers

Until your business has *drivers* (and *key drivers*) you're not going anywhere. The trouble lies in finding them. Drivers are not things that just anyone can see, so it is almost certain that you'll need a consultant. No one really knows why consultants can find them when no one else can, but it might be because it was a consultant who invented them.

There are other words for *driver*, such as *factor*, *influence*, *reason* and *cause*; but you can see the folly of using any of those simply by trying to write this sentence without *drivers* in it: 'Practical approaches for defining valued business outcomes coupled with clear monitoring of the drivers of those valued outcomes.' *Causes* or *reasons* might work, but the synergy would be pitiful. Something reassuring happens when you put *drivers* with *outcomes*, and it's no accident – they grew up together.

A bundle of drivers

Interestingly, in this particular study a wide variety of attributes contribute to the choice, but the seven key drivers remain the most important. Offered, or not, these seven key drivers directly affected the work choice that respondents made (ie full-time, part-time, own business, contract/consult, retire). These seven key drivers need to be offered as a 'bundle'.

The Evolving Workplace, Hudson Consulting

Drivers of delight

Key drivers of guest delight are attributes that have a surprise value and a direct relationship with customers' repeat visit intent and thus a business' overall success. It is an important strategic task to determine what those critical attributes are. The aim of this paper is to provide a method for identifying those key drivers that contribute to guest delight . . . Drawing from a sample of guests to a food and wine festival, this research purports a simple but inherently useful tool to identify key drivers of guest satisfaction and delight through four survey questions.

International Journal of Contemporary Hospitality Management

Drivers of loyalty

In many cases, simply understanding the key drivers of physician loyalty can help organizations improve relationships with medical staff . . . Drivers of physician loyalty range from basic operational efficiency to elaborate clinical joint ventures.

BNET Australia ('the GO To Place for Management')

Primordial drivers

Having heard the views of a person in authority on our city's competitiveness, we should now be better equipped to meet the challenges of addressing our weaknesses. This, afterall, is the primordial intent of this exercise. I must thank Dr. Federico Macaranas and his colleagues from the AIM, Policy Center for accommodating our request for a half-day seminar on Seven Key Drivers of Competitiveness. We are thankful for the efforts made by Dr. Macaranas to relate the key drivers to Marikina.

Vice Mayor's Closing Remarks. Seminar on Seven Key Drivers of Competitiveness, Shoe Hall, Marikina, Philippines, 22 September 2006

Drivers of results

VisionLink is a consulting firm located in Irvine, CA dedicated to helping companies envision, create and sustain compensation strategies that will be key drivers of results and increase the productivity of employees.

The VisionLink Advisory Group

Driven to satisfaction

The reasoning for this reflective summary is for you to evaluate your alignment with job enrichment (achieving high satisfaction in your place of work). For some this may involve seeking promotion whilst for others it may involve lateral transfer to one or more locations. It is your own reflection affected by your own career drivers (i.e. what drives you to satisfaction).

From a memo sent out to participants of a development program

Key Performance Indicators (KPIs)

Before KPIs the world was a very dark place. Nothing worked as well as it should. Most people were incompetent or drunk. There was very little going forward, and such progress as there was could not be measured. There were no consultants; at least, not enough to spoil the nicer suburbs. Where there was chaos KPIs brought whips, and to the darkness they brought scorpions.

> The Area Performance Agreement for chief executives says paying all creditors within the benchmark 45 days is a key performance indicator.
>
> *Canberra Times*

> We are looking for cows that calve annually in the first four weeks of the breeding season. Empty rates are 5 per cent, a key performance indicator for us.
>
> www.stuff.co.nz

> York VC has become the 40th club to achieve Volley 123 accreditation ensuring Volleyball England has met another Sport England Key Performance Indicator (KPI) well in advance of the final deadline of March 2009.
>
> www.volleyballengland.org

> The Waste Wise KPIs can be used to measure the effectiveness of the range of identified actions in each of the three levels of the Waste Wise program for local governments.
> Bronze: Achieving widespread participation and involvement
> Silver: Implementing improved practices and significant resource efficiency

Gold: Providing leadership and capacity building for continual improvement

The key actions provided in each table are recommendations for each corresponding level; however, key actions from other levels can be incorporated into your action plan — the different levels are not mutually exclusive.

Sustainability Victoria

On average, non-indigenous Australians live about as long as any group of people in the world, and each decade they live a few years longer. By contrast, Indigenous Australians can expect to die at much the same age as people in Turkmenistan and Bangladesh. Among Indigenous Australians, infant mortality is at least twice as high, and diabetes and cardiovascular disease six or seven times higher.

KPIs for the disadvantaged

Significantly, both DHF and non-government Health Services committed to working together, with agreement for DHF to facilitate development of the NTAHKPI Information System which provides:

- validated definitions for the agreed core suite of 19 KPIs

- a system for data collection, cleaning, analysis and interpretation and enables feedback at community level

- an NT jurisdiction wide system for reporting KPI data on Aboriginal health.

The Information Act and related Information Privacy Principles (Schedule 2 IPP 1 & 2) provide underpinning legislation regarding management of NTAHF KPI data held in the Data Warehouse.

In DHF Health Centres, the Primary Care Information System (PCIS) and the Interim Data Collection Tool facilitate KPI data collection for most of the KPIs in the Health Services domain . . .

Data Sponsor / Delegate: the person who undertakes the duties of ownership of a data collection under the control of DHF.

3. Responsibilities

3.1 Remote Health Branch Staff

- Be aware of the agreed KPIs and the NTAHKPI Information System

- Ensure relevant staff are adequately introduced to and utilise the method of data collection available in the Health Centre, eg PCIS, Interim Data Collection Tool

- Produce and utilise DHF KPI reports to support NT wide, regional and Health Centre planning

- Ensure relevant policies and protocols related to external application for access to data are followed as appropriate

Northern Territory Health Department

Imagine you are an Indigenous Australian. Someone has just read you this information from the Northern Territory Health Department. Do you now feel a) reassured, b) optimistic, c) bamboozled, or d) nothing?

Important enhancements to performance appraisal (having regard to feedback following roll-out)

After a period of review with a reference group of willing volunteers from across the different divisions, a number of important enhancements have been made to the Performance Appraisal process having regard to the feedback received from programs following initial roll out of the scheme in August last year.

E-newsletter from a human resources manager

Bench strength

The essential features of the scheme are:

- To provide a platform for building the capability of our workforce

- To increase the 'depth of talent' and 'bench strength' of capability for current and emerging workforce requirements

- To enhance work and business performance and productivity by developing skills and behaviours that are essential for current and future success.

E-newsletter from a human resources manager

KPI for drive strategy (tractor)

As a general rule, it is possible to say of this engine speed reduction function that it serves as a key indicator for the drive strategy.

Case CVX 195 Tractor Operator's Manual

LAA indicators agreed by GOSE

Performance Management

5.1: The 198 indicators in the new National Indicator Set will be collected and performance managed through PB Views Performance Management System which is being used by local authorities within Berkshire. The new National Indicator Set replaces the previous Best Value Performance Indicators. The LAA (Local Area Agreement) indicators have been selected

from the National Indicator Set and agreed by GOSE.
The agreed list was published at the end of May.
The Council will be assessed against its performance
against all 198 indicators through the Use of Resources
Assessment . . .

Slough Borough Council

Get your outturns in the members' room

A report detailing the Best Value Performance
Indicator outturns for 2007/08 was published on
June 30th and is available in the members' room.
Alternatively a copy can be obtained from the Policy
and Performance Team . . .

Slough Borough Council

Advanced KPIs

If You Build It, Will They Come?

Could you – should you – offer to custom-build real-
time KPI digital dashboards for every C-level executive
in your firm? Would they be thrilled, indifferent to,
or insulted by your offer?'

Michael Schrage, 6 October 2004

At Microsoft's CEO summit in May, the software
giant's own CEO, Steve Ballmer, spoke passionately
about the importance of having 'digital dashboards':
real-time desktop displays of key performance
indicators (KPIs) that show critical business ratios
such as profit per sales employee per week, customer
satisfaction in dispute resolution and the status of
outstanding issues with major suppliers.

www.cio.com.au

Buy-in

Buy-in is a bit like *uptake* (see below). It is required of just about everybody because just about everybody is a customer. But we also want *buy-in* from *our people* – in fact, they're not really our people until we have it from them. When our people 'buy' our vision, we have *buy-in* – which means we *have* our people.

Strategic use of *key enablers* – such as bonuses, promotions, flattery or celebrations of *achieved key benchmarks* – enable us to achieve buy-in through buy-off. Tell them a story – a really good one – and give them a reward for listening to it. Spin it like gossamer around their poor Pavlovian minds. Soon they'll spin it back to you, and with a crafty system of rewards in place they'll spin it with more conviction than even you could bring to it.

If after all this you still don't get buy-in, you might be tempted to think there's something wrong with the vision. No way. Remember, you put your arse into that thing: it's a cultural issue. You can't run a business with all the essential values of diversity, flexibility and agility if you've got renegades trotting round with their own agendas. Liquidate all counter-revolutionary elements! 'Buy-in or #★@&-off!' is the fallback for every good business process.

Powerful tool

Call Evelyn Clark now to discuss how she can help you add the powerful tool of storytelling to your tool kit.

www.corpstory.com

Agreeance on extrapulation

Thanks. I am in total agreeance with you. I'll ensure that we extrapulate the core season items to create a story. Can you ensure that the price points reflect our aspirational client's goal sets.

Salco Manufacturing, March 2007

Facilitating the objective-setting process

The role of the Liaison Librarians project team is to:
Facilitate the objective-setting process, work with
those in similar roles to reach consensus on role-
specific objectives and KPIs, obtain buy-in from
stakeholders during the planning process by seeking
feedback, reporting back to stakeholders, keep in mind
the overall aim of the objective-setting process.

Internal memo of the University of Sydney Library

Flyers buy-in/Buyers fly in

Within the city and its environs there exists a core
strength of difference and diversity . . . As a more
culturally and ethnically diverse and design-aware
traveller takes to the skies, 'intangible' factors are
increasingly driving consumer buy-in.

The Future Laboratory Melbourne Retail Strategy

Community buy-in

So this is more about pulling this work together and
making it public in a way that the community can have
buy in, so they can see that we're serious about doing
anything we can.

ACT Health Minister, Katy Gallagher

Ideological glue

The corporate bonding glue will increasingly become
ideological. People still have a fundamental need for
guiding values and a sense of purpose that gives their
life and work meaning.

Jim Collins and Jerry I. Porras, authors of *Built to Last: Successful Habits of
Visionary Companies*

Software buy-in

Once you physically install Sage Accpac ERP you have
reached a critical stage in the adoption of your new
software by employees, and you need to create employee
'buy in' to ensure that the Sage Accpac is being adopted
and used efficiently across your organization . . . The
more an employee uses the software the more they take
ownership and 'buy in' to the software.

www.accpac.net.au

Embedded and enhanced buy-in

11:30–12:30 Building on the strategic capabilities of your employees

Design and implement a capability framework which is:

- Relevant to all employees
- Responsive to the organisation's business needs
- Embracing of organisational values

Discover successful communication strategies to
enhance employee 'buy-in' and embed the new
behaviours into employees' daily routines.

Mark Harris, educational leader, Southbank Institute of Technology

Buying buy-in

Here are a few starting points to help leaders begin a
process that results in employee buy-in:

- Create the vision by telling a company story that
  sets the rationale – the economic, psychological and
  moral imperative to fulfill this vision.

- Foster excitement, motivation, and engagement
  around the vision by articulating the WIFM (What's
  In It For Me) factor.

- Let your employees know how they will benefit from embracing the vision. Explain and reinforce the financial rewards when the goals of the vision have been achieved, such as bonuses, recognition, and career development . . .

- Develop visuals, such as tables, charts and photos, which highlight milestone accomplishments of the vision.

- Create and align company goals with the vision, and align individual and team goals with company goals.

- Identify a cross-functional change management team that can anticipate the impact of the vision . . .

- Talk it up . . .

- Celebrate meaningful benchmarks along the way.

'Get employee buy-in for your vision', Bonni Carson Dimatteo

Buy-in by any other name

Instead of a roadshow it should be referred to as the employee stakeholder engagement initiative.

So the focus for the next phase in terms of emphasis should be explaining:

- our commitment to Australia

- who we are and what are our values

- clarifying and refining the distribution channel strategy

Its important to reshape Graham's messaging as he is coming across as being too waffly. He hasn't taken on board our training sessions at all.

Also I had lunch with Jenny and she is feeling loved and engaged and is now back in the loop. She is going to input into the channel manuals.

Also I'm going to be offline from now as I'm going back to the hotel before I catch up with some people later on from HP and PWC.

Weasel Words website. The listener explains 'This person is, of course, *hot-desking* from out of town . . .'

Uptake

You can have the best product on the planet but you're sunk without *uptake*. We pinched the word from scientists who used it to describe things like glucose in muscle cells and arsenic in fish, and that's as good a reason as any for preferring it to *adopt, use, buy, pay for, accept, employ, absorb, welcome* or *take* – they're so unscientific. The same goes for *gulled, conned, defraud* and *fell for it*, of course. *Uptake* is the one you want. Try to use it as a noun, but *verbing* it every now and then – like, 'Do we have a ballpark on how many are likely to uptake this offer?' – can win a certain regard among more credulous employees. *Take-up* is acceptable, but a little obscure.

Business owners report low kiwisaver uptake.

Grant Thornton NZ

Manager of uptake

The State Services Commission has appointed a Business Development and Uptake Manager to support SSC's new role as a provider of mission-critical all-of-government services.

www.e.govt.nz

Driver of uptake

Roisin King, who has extensive experience in IT service sales and management, will be responsible for driving the services uptake to achieve the necessary subscription for the SSC's suite of products and services, including the Government Shared Network and the Government Logon Service.

www.e.govt.nz

Uptake around the corner

Though many industry stakeholders have predicted a long winter for the Indian offshoring industry, research firm Everest Group believes an uptake is around the corner . . . 'We are seeing a lot of activity in people,' Mr Samuel told *Business Line* in a recent interview.

Hindu Business Line

Achieving high uptake

Despite a concentration of risk factors for HIV transmission, many remote Aboriginal communities in central Australia have a low uptake of HIV testing. We studied the uptake of HIV testing in six clinics in remote Aboriginal communities following the introduction of voluntary confidential testing to assess the impact of the intervention and to determine if the program was reaching people most at risk of HIV infection and transmission . . .
This study shows that a high uptake of HIV testing in high-risk groups can be achieved in remote Aboriginal communities where a high level of confidentiality is maintained.

Australian and New Zealand Journal of Public Health

Various other uptakes

Schools urged to talk business to improve languages uptake.

Aston University Birmingham, United Kingdom

Business networks and the uptake of sustainability practices: the case of New Zealand.

University of Waikato

Consumer take-up of Windows Vista will far outstrip business take-up in terms of their share of the market, said analyst IDC.

www.computerweekly.com

One possible result of water extraction is the uptake of fish, particularly juveniles.

www.nzsteel.co.nz

Outcomes

Imagine a world without outcomes, in which all input is meaningless, solutions unknown and utilisation of output unimplementable. Such a world would be a black hole for all stakeholders. Believe it or not, just two decades ago the world was not *outcomes-based*. There were *consequences, effects, results, eventualities, repercussions, corollaries, by-products, sequels, conclusions, harvests, aftermaths, denouements, offspring* and *outgrowths*, all of them milling about and taking up valuable space. How do you measure those? You can't. But outcomes you can measure; and when you can't, with a little shuffling of the categories, you can.

It's brilliant – especially in schools. With *outcomes-based education*, illiterate kids in the Northern Territory can get a B in English. Outcomes-based education is *total quality management* for schools: it puts them on a sort of scientific basis, and that's got to be good, even if the science is bogus and no one understands what's going on. Now the whole world works on an outcomes-based basis, and if you can't see the benefits you have no business being in business, or being a school teacher, or a doctor or anything.

Can anyone think of a more satisfying outcome?

Solution

We created a tailored senior leadership program for the AFL. A five-and-a-half day residential business program, the initiative covers leadership, marketing, financial management, brand management, strategy and negotiation.

Outcome

AFL staff applied their learnings through projects that directly benefit the organisation. These include projects on the AFL's match day experience, its international strategy, corporate social responsibility plan and brand strategy.

Mount Eliza Executive Education

Issues and gaps

A desired outcome from the workshop was to achieve a better understanding of the relationship between the insurance/risk industry and the spatial industry and identify issues and gaps, and the development of an action plan to progress understanding in this area.

WALIS Advisory Committee (WAC)

Outcomes from utilised outputs

Project outcomes are achieved from the utilisation of the outputs delivered by a project. Not to be confused with Agency Budget Outcomes and treasury arrangements.

Tasmanian Government

No right turn outcome

Turning right into the carpark is prohibited due to the high risk assessment outcomes.

From a Worksafe (Victoria) information sheet about 'accessing the Training Centre at the Preston Office'

Stimulating outcome

Of equal importance was the need to share the outcomes of projects in order to stimulate further adoption of the innovation . . .

The Smart Water Fund

Enhanced outcomes in addressing issues with MSPs

Offering communities enhanced outcomes in addressing sustainability issues is an emergent collaborative model integrating knowledge, competencies and resources from diverse organisations – multi-stakeholder partnerships (MSP).

Commentary: Sustainability and Innovation, CSIRO, 2007

Community outcomes ensure outcomes for the community

2.2 Value and support families to improve community development outcomes by investing in the early years to ensure enhanced outcomes for the community.

Strategic Plan for Burnie, Tasmania, May 2006

Measurably better (and improved) outcomes

In her Ministerial Statement of May 2004, the Minister for Community Services identified three key objectives to guide reform of children's and family services in Victoria. These were to:

- create one integrated system for children and families based on shared responsibility and mutual accountability

- focus that system on promoting children's wellbeing and safety in the broader context of children's developmental needs

- produce measurably better outcomes for children and improved system outcomes

Victorian Government report

Thinking converted into outcomes

eighthgate is CitiPower and Powercor's Innovation Initiative. It is a conduit for unlocking and fostering innovative thinking, with true entrepreneurial spirit, and converting that thinking into outcomes.

Powercor.com.au

Outcomes you can sing

The intention is to make clear the ambitions of council to enable us to provide better outcomes for our communities, essentially so that we are all singing from the same hymn book.

hepburn.yourguide.com.au

Blending outcomes

Luminosity blends strategic, creative and technical minds to deliver successful outcomes through targeted visual communication. Working closely

with our clients, we develop brand identities,
corporate publications, advertising and marketing
communications, internet applications, and related
e-business solutions.

> Luminosity

Outcomes-based drug prices

Rather than coming at the tail end of a drug's
development, pricing planning is being integrated
into drug development. The pricing department,
in fact, is now a key driver in lifecycle management.
Outcomes-Based Pharmaceutical Pricing: Meeting Stakeholder Needs
examines these industry trends. It provides action
items to resolve pricing departments' most pressing
problems.

> Cutting Edge Information

Tail outcome

I do not know anyone who predicted this course of
events. This should give us cause to reflect on how
hard a job it is to make genuinely useful forecasts.
What we have seen is truly a 'tail' outcome – the kind
of outcome that the routine forecasting process never
predicts. But it has occurred, it has implications, and
so we must reflect on it.

> From 'Interesting Times', a speech by Glenn Stevens, governor of the Reserve Bank,
> 9 December 2008

Targeted plan outcomes

The 2005-2007 plan is based on a revised business
model which recognises the market focus of the
organisation and aligns relevant activities to ensure
that we maximise the level of collaboration to achieve
the targeted plan outcomes. This has required a

refocusing of our current organisational structure
(Refer Appendix A) to comprise three core business
groups and a CEO directed support unit comprising
marketing, HR and special projects.

From a document released by EAN Australia in 2004

Education outcomes

Education Queensland promotes the practices and
philosophy of 'Outcomes Based Education'. O.B.E.
places the learner and their needs as the 'hub' of
Curriculum planning and teaching methods used in
our lessons. We may well claim that this is nothing new
for effective teachers and this may be true, however . . .
Lessons can now be directed towards assisting students
in developing specific identified outcomes (per
syllabus) utilizing whatever context we believe best
suites outcome development and student interest.

Work programs are likely to be less content focussed
and more 'skill' focussed with more room for student
negotiation.

Enhanced student performance is anticipated as
students become more engaged in areas of interest and
their own learning.

Toowoomba Curriculum Exchange

An enabling strategy for a learning outcome

Some business language defies categorisation: not because
there's any shortage of *event chain methodologies* or *revolving
enablers*, but because any more than a couple of them on the
same page invites madness. Read these random examples.
Take your time. Let them seep into your brain. Then adapt a

favourite paragraph or verse to the management style. Try for instance, the opening paragraph of *Pride and Prejudice*, *The Man from Snowy River*, *The Owl and the Pussycat*, Kipling's *If*.

Increasingly more

. . . a look-forward meeting to discuss and evaluate the company's event-chain methodology . . . You should all be proud of the amount of effort and energy you have put forth thus far, and can be certain the project's conclusion will become more apparent as the tasks become increasingly more finite.

Project manager, MediaLine

Seamless

Suggestions for enhancing synergies across seamless boundaries.

Notice on a suggestion box

Aggressive paradigms

Petrobras has established new global benchmarks for the generation of exceptional shareholder wealth through an aggressive and innovative programme of cost cutting on its P36 production facility. Conventional constraints have been successfully challenged and replaced with new paradigms appropriate to the globalised corporate market place.

Press release from Petrobas, 2004

Get revenue focussed

Our theme for the next six months is to become more revenue focused. Every choice of action should be judged by which will most positively affect the companies revenue.

Email to all Fairfax staff, 29 July 2005

Revolving enablers

The enablers revolve around the creation of a fund level data store at a level of detail that will support the sort of drill downs specified in the data framework referred to above, including individual details. Above this will be a datamart derived from the data store and aggregated to a level that supports the types of analyses the client requires to identify trends or segregate segments and clusters. The use of aggregated data to establish segments and clusters and to identify trends will offer favourable response times by narrowing the amount of data to be churned in the interrogation and filtering process.

> Memorandum sent by a superannuation administration company, Melbourne

Deconditioned yet interested

Health clubs have rarely penetrated this deconditioned, yet interested market as their market penetration percentage hovers in the mid teens.

> www.gymlink.co.nz

Connecting with the base, not

'It was a commercial decision, as *The Footy Show* in its current format does not allow us to connect well with the customer base,' an ANZ spokeswoman told *The Melbourne Age*.

> ANZ announces it will no longer sponsor *The Footy Show*

In this message, *current format* means Sam Newman; *does not allow us to connect well* means insults, offends, etc.; and *customer base* means a lot of women. They would have said they made the decision 'because Sam Newman insults a lot of women', but that might have been taken to mean they were concerned for the feelings of the women. Then all the other stakeholders might have said it was not a commercial decision and felt as offended as the women.

Knee causes issues

Lance's knee has been causing issues . . .

A football coach. The issues have caused Lance to retire.

Recoveries executed

Empowering people to execute remarkable recoveries that ensure total guest satisfaction.

One of the top ten values from a Legion and Community club members handbook

Turn key paradigm

The GRAVITY SYSTEM is a revolutionary turn key business paradigm you use to consistently draw new interest and attract greater profits . . . Encircling the GRAVITY SYSTEM are the four disciplines that drive profits your way – groups strength classes, Pilates, personal training, and post rehab – all on the GTS machine, your premium space utilizer.

www.genofit.com

Reverse brief event

Explanation of 'reverse brief'

The words 'reverse brief' referred to in Reference Group correspondence appear to be being used to describe a possible redefinition of the master plan focus and a redesign of its fundamental brief.

This is not the genesis or the context of the expression 'reverse brief', in this instance.

Due to the nature of Prof. Paul Carter's presentation to us we requested he provide us with a

'reverse brief' to better articulate his
professional services and allow us to negotiate a
scope of work.

Whilst his work will hopefully result in a profoundly
improved foundation for the master planning, the
expression 'reverse brief' merely describes the process
of communication for now.

In respect of the concern's of XXX, manifestation
of Material Thinking's concepts are fundamental
to their appointment and will be monitored closely
through the delivery.

Weasel Words website

Group efficiency beliefs

Collective Cognition in Action: Accumulation,
Interaction, Examination, and Accommodation in the
Development and Operation of Group Efficacy Beliefs
in the Workplace.

Title from a recent paper from the *Academy of Management Review*

Right-shoring

Business shouldn't look at 'right-shoring' as
establishing a vendor partnership, he said. Instead,
they should see the chance to use 'constituents' to help
deliver that work.

Chris Mitchell, local managing director of EDS (an 'outsourcing giant'), telling 'top
bankers that offshoring more backoffice operations was the answer to remaining
competitive'

Buzzwords to capture target market

In our experience . . . we have found that using
'buzzwords' are a great way to capture our target market
as this is the language that they use within their jobs
every day. I allocated a lot of time during my research

to investigate and understand the 'buzzwords' that our target audience uses and recognises most.

Conference organiser quoted on www.employee-communication.com.au

His product has gone up into a different gear.

Channel 7 tennis commentator

Markets

People who do not know the market, or play or ride it, might assume it is incapable of ordinary human feeling. Not so. Having to do with money, it shares something of money's character, which the young Karl Marx called 'the alienated ability of mankind'. Were we to accept this, we might see the market as this 'alienated ability' made animate, and those who wrestle with it as in some sense wrestling with themselves. Before you dismiss this characterisation as altogether too silly, watch Jim Cramer on CNBC: that might not be his alienated self he's wrestling with, but it's someone very close to him.

Those who know the market have often ascribed to it a quasi-religious dimension. For a very long portion of the history of capitalism it shared a close relationship with Providence. In a famous phrase beloved of free marketeers, Adam Smith said that when men were allowed to pursue their own self-interest, society was governed by a generally benevolent 'invisible hand'. Smith's 'hand' was God's, 'whose wisdom works itself through competition for wealth'; but the true modern market disciple reckons it a blasphemy to think the hand could belong to anyone or anything but the market.

Listen to them for a while and you would swear the 'invisible hand' was the least of the market's mysterious properties. The thing has a sort of animal intelligence, corresponding perhaps to that of a Doberman or grey parrot. The market sees things, it senses things, it sulks, it anticipates, it gets depressed, it has friends, it is inscrutable: it understands things that we mortals do not.

This market is sick of the leadership; not of the stocks like General Electric (GE:NYSE) and Microsoft (MSFT:Nasdaq), but of the president and the vice president, and nothing that comes out this week or the next or the week after in earnings will change that.

Jim Cramer, CNBC

I wanted to believe that he could articulate correctly why we went to war in some foreign land where a thousand guys have died and billions have been spent. But he hasn't. He had terrible intelligence and bad homework, stuff I fire people for regularly and always have . . . The market senses this, and that casts a pall over every day's trading.

Jim Cramer, CNBC

What we see now in the market is a gradual realization that Bush will be forced out in November and a new man will be president . . .

Jim Cramer, CNBC

I know that President George W. Bush has been a good friend of the market when it comes to taxing those of us with lots of money. We've done great these last few years. But it is time to recognize that things aren't working. Time to recognize that the stock market is out of favor because we don't trust it, and that the trust is more a function of the leadership in Washington than it is of anything the companies have to say.

Jim Cramer, CNBC

Markets cause slowdown

The political process started in late 2007. Since that time, the markets have been down 55 percent. Markets are forward-looking, not backward-looking. They saw what was coming in the election. They were anticipating what this guy would do, and they caused a slowdown.

Art Laffer, CNBC, March 2009

Markets fail to understand

Distressed Securities: Buys equity, debt, or trade claims at deep discounts of companies in or facing bankruptcy or reorganization. Profits from the market's lack of understanding of the true value of the deeply discounted securities and because the majority of institutional investors cannot own below investment grade securities. (This selling pressure creates the deep discount.) Results generally not dependent on the

direction of the markets. Expected Volatility: Low –
Moderate

www.magnum.com

Market up, market down

The [Bernie Madoff] strategy is generally described
as putting on a 'collar' in an attempt to limit gains
compared to the benchmark index in an up market
and, likewise, limit losses to something less than the
benchmark in a down market, essentially creating a
floor and a ceiling.

MAR/Hedge (RIP) No. 89, May 2001

Markets sideways

On top of experiencing relatively weak investment
returns in sideways markets, hedge fund investors have
many important issues to consider as we enter 2003,
including conflicts of interest, regulation, style drift,
opacity and capacity constraints.

9th Annual Hedge Fund Managers' Conference, Phoenix, Arizona 2003

Markets not crazy

You can say on one hand the market is crazy but
it's not 1999. People have had their medicine from
overexuberance.

James Packer

Flipside of downside

In our base case simulation there is an upside case that,
er, corresponds on the flipside of the downside case in
kind of an adverse direction.

A World Bank economist, 2008

Nature's downtick

[It's] human nature, wanting to get that last downtick.

Bob Griffeth, CNBC, March 2009

Hiney in the innovation tent

Once the Federal government gets both its regulatory nose, and its bureaucratic hiney, in the innovation tent, a series of irrevocable events will take place that foreclose future innovation economic growth.

Thomas E. Vass

Market matures into granularity

The key concept is that of risk assessment, and this is becoming more granular by nature as the market matures. The question is, does the industry have the datasets required to drill down into to get the level of granularity required for this and, more importantly, are the data accessible to the industry.

Wallis Advisory Committee

Market without hiney

The only way that has ever been discovered to have a lot of people cooperate together voluntarily is through the free market. And that's why it's so essential to preserving individual freedom.

Milton Friedman

Liberals and pedants might ask if people do not 'cooperate together' in religion, field games, war, mothers' clubs and disasters; if they did not 'cooperate together' to split the atom; and isn't everybody now cooperating together to rescue the market before it dies by its own invisible hand? Silly people.

Alan Greenspan

Not everyone in this life has a put named after him. But Alan Greenspan has the Greenspan Put. What seems strange to people who don't have a put named after them – who would not recognise a put if they stepped on one – is why, when the market possesses a thing as wonderful as an 'invisible hand', it needs a put like the Greenspan Put. What sort of invisible hand can't keep a reliable grip on asset prices? One would think that it could generate its own liquidity, and even manage its own risk.

But these are the wrong questions! The market fails us because *we* have been bad. With our ignorance and doubt and base presumption, it is clear we have offended the invisible hand. We must make an atonement. And if that takes a put, so be it. Trouble is, every time we send up a successful offering it gets factored into asset prices and the credit spreads are narrowed.

> Any onset of increased investor caution elevates
> risk premiums and, as a consequence, lowers asset
> values and promotes the liquidation of the debt that
> supported higher asset prices.
>
> August 2005

No government regulation necessary

> Risk in financial markets, including derivatives
> markets, are being regulated by private
> parties . . . There is nothing involved in federal
> regulation per se which makes it superior to market
> regulation. The risk of a crisis stoked by loose
> derivative trading was extremely remote.
>
> 1994

Risks hedged

I believe that the general
growth in large institutions
have occurred in the context
of an underlying structure of
markets in which many
of the larger risks are
dramatically – I should say,
fully – hedged.

2000

No worries

Perhaps the most significant innovation has been the
development of financial instruments that enable risk
to be reallocated to the parties most willing and able
to bear that risk. Many of the new financial products
that have been created, with financial derivatives
being the most notable, contribute economic value
by unbundling risks and shifting them in a highly
calibrated manner.

April 2000

Under control

Building on bank practice, we are in the process of
improving both lending and supervisory policies that
we trust will foster better risk management; but these
policies could also reduce the pro-cyclical pattern of
easing and tightening of bank lending and accordingly
increase bank shareholder values and economic
stability. It is not an easy road, but it seems that we are
well along it.

June 2001

Innovation has taken care of it

In recent years, we have incorporated innovative ideas
and accommodated significant change in banking and
supervision. Institutions have more ways than ever
to compete in providing financial services. Financial
innovation has improved the measurement and
management of risk and holds substantial promise for
much greater gains ahead.

June 2001

Don't worry – new paradigms

The development of our paradigms for containing
risk has emphasized, and will, of necessity, continue
to emphasize dispersion of risk to those willing,
and presumably able, to bear it. If risk is properly
dispersed, shocks to the overall economic system will
be better absorbed and less likely to create cascading
failures that could threaten financial stability . . .

September 2002

Only a fool would regulate

But regulation is not only unnecessary in these
markets, it is potentially damaging, because regulation
presupposes disclosure and forced disclosure of
proprietary information can undercut innovations in
financial markets just as it would in real estate markets.

September 2002

It's taken care of, I tell you

A major contributor to the dispersion of risk
in recent decades has been the wide-ranging
development of markets in securitized bank loans,
credit card receivables, and commercial and
residential mortgages. These markets have tailored

the risks associated with holding such assets to fit the preferences of a broader spectrum of investors.

September 2002

Relax ...

Especially important in the United States has been the flexibility and size of the secondary mortgage market. Since early 2000, this market has facilitated the large debt-financed extraction of home equity that, in turn, has been so critical in supporting consumer outlays in the United States throughout the recent period of cyclical stress. This market's flexibility has been particularly enhanced by extensive use of interest rate swaps and options to hedge maturity mismatches and prepayment risk.

September 2002

Absolutely no worries

In conjunction with this improvement, both as cause and effect, banks have more tools at their disposal with which to transfer credit risk and, in so doing, to disperse credit risk more broadly through the financial system. Some of these tools, such as loan syndications, loan sales, and pooled asset securitizations, are relatively straightforward and transparent. More recently, instruments that are more complex and less transparent — such as credit default swaps, collateralized debt obligations, and credit-linked notes — have been developed and their use has grown very rapidly in recent years. The result? Improved credit-risk management together with more and better risk-management tools appear to have significantly reduced loan concentrations in telecommunications and, indeed, other areas and the associated stress on banks and other financial institutions.

November 2002

The market has it well in hand

What we have found over the years in the marketplace is that derivatives have been an extraordinarily useful vehicle to transfer risk from those who shouldn't be taking it to those who are willing to and are capable of doing so. It would be a mistake to increase regulation.

2003

The strategy is working

Instead of trying to contain a putative bubble by drastic actions with largely unpredictable consequences, we chose . . . to focus on policies to mitigate the fallout when it occurs and, hopefully, ease the transition to the next expansion . . . There appears to be enough evidence, at least tentatively, to conclude that our strategy of addressing the bubble's consequences rather than the bubble itself has been successful.

2004

How many times do I have to tell you?

. . . private regulation generally has proved far better at constraining excessive risk-taking than has government regulation . . .

May 2005

There could be a problem or two . . .

The rapid proliferation of derivatives products inevitably means that some will not have been adequately tested by market stress. Even with sound credit-risk management, a sudden widening of credit spreads could result in unanticipated losses to investors in some of the newer, more complex structured credit products, and those investors could include some leveraged hedge funds.

May 2005

But I'm pretty sure the market . . .

Risk management involves judgment as well as science, and the science is based on the past behavior of markets, which is not an infallible guide to the future. Yet the history of the development of these products encourages confidence that many of the newer products will be successfully embraced by the markets. To be sure, for that favorable record to be extended, both market participants and policymakers must be aware of the risk-management challenges associated with the use of derivatives to transfer risk, both within the banking system and outside the banking system. And they must take steps to ensure that those challenges are addressed.

May 2005

In any case the benefits outweigh . . .

With these advances in technology, lenders have taken advantage of credit-scoring models and other techniques for efficiently extending credit to a broader spectrum of consumers. The widespread adoption of these models has reduced the costs of evaluating the creditworthiness of borrowers, and in competitive markets cost reductions tend to be passed through to borrowers. Where once more-marginal applicants would simply have been denied credit, lenders are now able to quite efficiently judge the risk posed by individual applicants and to price that risk appropriately. These improvements have led to rapid growth in subprime mortgage lending.

April 2005

Hang on . . .

'I have found a flaw. I don't know how significant or permanent it is.

'I made a mistake in presuming that the self-interests of organizations, specifically banks and others, were such as that they were best capable of protecting their own shareholders and their equity in the firms . . . But I have been very distressed by that fact . . .'

'In other words, you found that your view of the world, your ideology, was not right, it was not working,' Mr. Waxman said.

'Absolutely, precisely,' Mr. Greenspan replied. 'You know, that's precisely the reason I was shocked, because I have been going for 40 years or more with very considerable evidence that it was working exceptionally well.

'The problem here is something that looked to be a very solid edifice . . . did break down. And I think that, as I said, shocked me. I still do not fully understand why it happened.'

October 2008

Leveraging

Time was when greedy and necessitous people sold their grandmothers: but only a fool would do that now when we can *leverage* her. There are other words for it: *utilise, exploit, gear, make the most of, take advantage of, use common sense – alchemy, the transmutation of souls –* but none of them holds a candle to *leveraging* your *global footprint* or your *mobility pie*. It is essential to get a handle on *leverage* and all the ingenious leveraging products that let you turn debt into equity, borrowings into fortunes and losses into total wipeouts.

Should you find your leveraging gives you spasms of guilt – the name can't disguise the fact you're doing something your father said you shouldn't – never forget that leveraging is as natural to human beings as sex and avarice. Leverage is one of the things that got the human race upright and going forwards, and instinct has been telling us ever since that moment in evolution to seek similar opportunities. Weep and hang your head in shame by all means. Go ahead, leverage your feelings – leverage them unto closure, if you like.

Guess

What makes a well educated veteran who lived through the Long Term Capital melt-down ten years ago think nothing of leveraging forty-to-one a portfolio of sub-prime paper backed by overpriced houses next to Interstate 80 in Sacramento?

From the 'Jeff Matthews Is Not Making This Up' blog

How it works

This is how it works: a securitisation includes a BBB tranche of say $10 million. New CDOs are put together in which each CDO buys $10 million worth of protection (insurance) on this tranche, usually from hedge funds. There are underlying Mortgage pools out there with Credit Default exposures literally tens of times their underlying size. Admittedly, the losses on the CDOs are offset by profits to hedge funds, but that's cold comfort to the leveraged owners of the CDOs.

Letter to *The New York Times*, 28 December 2007

Doing it with water

The aim was to leverage innovation embedded in frustrated stakeholders who needed support to pursue opportunities to take a leadership role in water conservation.

The Smart Water Fund

With science

Prominence of the need to harness cross-organisation capability (scale and assembly of complementary capabilities), leveraging the significant strategic differentiation from cross-discipline and cross-boundary activities in line with our chosen strategic direction, as articulated in our 03/07 Strategic Plan.

From the CSIRO's Executive Management Committee's Science Investment Process 'Broad Direction Setting' document

Enhancing it

The 'structured credit' fund was the model for the 'enhanced leverage' fund.

Business Week, 12 June 2007

A Headshift persepective

From a Headshift perspective, Web 2.0 technologies are very much about leveraging the natural dynamics of an organisation and matching them with social software to facilitate a collaboration process that helps organisations meet their business objectives . . .

Livio Hughes, co-founder and director of Headshift

Thoroughly magnanimous leverage

We did a review last year and decided that we should specifically target our community outlook to the environment. Our core business remains vehicle finance and given the impact vehicles have on the environment, we are committed to leveraging our strengths as an organisation to give back to the environment.

Preston Leader, 7 September 2004

Leverage lure

Over past decades of stock investment, I made lots of mistakes before, speculation and losses at earlier years, misjudgment of stock analysis, etc. But my net worth was never wiped out before because I have always been aware of the danger of margin and danger of leverage lure.

Henry Lu, www.blastinvest.com

A serious bit of leveraging

Based on the derivative side of its books, Long Term Capital had an astoundingly high debt-to-capital ratio. 'The off-balance sheet leverage was 100 to 1 or 200 to 1 — I don't know how to calculate it,' Peter Fisher, a senior Fed official, told Greenspan and other Fed governors at a Sept. 29, 1998, meeting.

The Washington Post, 15 October 2008

Life after leverage

Leverage Your Life is a group discussion series produced by Priority Associates. The series is designed to equip professionals to multiply their lives by building up others spiritually. Helping people come to Christ, developing them to spiritual maturity and watching them influence others spiritually is a profoundly fulfilling experience. Being involved in discipleship and spiritual multiplication takes time, energy and even sacrifice. However, the joy of seeing many lives changed for eternity is indeed worth the investment.

Campus Crusade for Christ

Unable to leverage closeness

You cannot leverage off your closeness to the President if the President values you to the extent that he couldn't be bothered spending any more than the minimum time with you.

The Australian, 28 March 2009

Australians all let us leverage off each other

There need to be a coordinated, integrated approach which will see the marketing efforts of all Australian businesses, artists, musicians, actors, sportspeople, designers and more, leverage off each other, under a united Australian brand.

Christopher Brown, Tourism and Transport Forum, *The Age*, June 2009

Rewrite the following sentences without using *leverage*

1. The show has even garnered some heavyweight support from the likes of the Australian Ballet's artistic director, David McAllister. 'The new dance TV shows

are leveraging the existing levels of interest, which have always been perhaps under-acknowledged,' he says.

The Australian, 28 March 2009

2. The DaVinci Method details how you can leverage your personality type the same way all great entrepreneurs have, leading to health, wealth and happiness.

The Da Vinci Method

3. Leverage Your Business Lunches To Maximize Your Sales Results.

www.evancarmichael.com

4. Leverage Your Experience: Turn your history into your future. His mission is to assist others who would desire to leverage their accumulated experience and to transform it into a 'second 50' year activity — whether for fun or for profit!

www.leverageyourexperience. com

5. Leverage your Distributed DB2 Skills to Get Started on DB2 UDB for the iSeries (AS/400).

www.silicon.com

6. Leverage your human resources function to improve performance now.

RSM McGladrey

7. There is a realization of capability in other parts of the services that we need to leverage.

US Navy Rear Admiral David Gove

8. Australia is really good at leveraging all its ethnic communities to create an Australian way of life. I think

there is a fantastic can-do spirit and a very healthy level of the entrepreneurial.

Tyler Brulee, *Belle*, July–August 2004

Complete the following sentences

Building and leveraging communities of practice . . .

Leverage your human resources function . . .

Leverage your own Creativity . . .

Leverage your Corporate Blogging Strategy . . .

Leverage your charitable gift . . .

The good that leveraging can do

Through the AIG Corporate Giving Program, we leverage our business expertise to contribute to economic growth and enhance civic life in the communities in which we operate.

AIG website

Washington DC, 9 February 2006: 'The Securities and Exchange Commission announced today the filing and settlement of charges that American International Group, Inc. (AIG) committed securities fraud. The settlement is part of a global resolution of federal and state actions under which AIG will pay in excess of $1.6 billion to resolve claims related to improper accounting, bid rigging and practices involving workers' compensation funds.'

AIG was recently ranked number 8 on a list of 655 bad-faith insurers. Up to its chin in credit swaps, it went under in the financial collapse, but refloated with the help of a $150 billion government bailout, of which it spent $165 million on executive 'retention payments'.

Deleveraging

I think basically what the figures indicate is that once you get households and businesses deleveraging there's a limit to what policy can do. Basically that deleveraging has to run its course and what policy can do is speed that adjustment and there is every indication it's working.

Paul Brennan, head of economics at Citigroup

Well, would you?

Would you like to negotiate and influence your capability to the next level of your current level of expertise? . . . develop personal behavioural flexibility, distinguish between process and content and understand where and how to leverage both.

'Negotiation and Influencing for Business Results', an Australian Marketing and Social Research Society event

Only the leveraged shall enter

The hard sell continued, with potential clients who lacked any capacity to borrow 'filtered out' of the education sessions. Those who were able to 'use leverage to maximise investment capacity' were brought into the Storm family. 'One of the core components of Storm's model is to create wealth for clients by accessing their full investment capacity, rather than simply manage their existing wealth,' said documents accompanying Storm's aborted sharemarket listing.

The Age, 17 January 2009

Tooth leverage

The first brush with Smart Technology to inspire patients to become more passionate about oral care. Leverages clinically proven oscillating-rotating technology. An advanced new brush head takes cleaning performance to the next level. The combination of innovative technology and design delivers the dramatic results your patients are looking for to keep them motivated.

Advertisement for an electric toothbrush

Products, hedges, alpha, etc.

This is the high end of it all, what really smart people have been doing with themselves for the past couple of decades. Ask yourself: while they've been *generating alpha*, what have you been generating? If the answer is something other than alpha, or if you don't know what *eases heteroskedacity*, don't imagine you're going to understand anything on the next couple of pages. Of course, you might say the people who wrote this stuff didn't understand it either — but what was *your* retention payment last year?

9th Annual Hedge Fund Investors' Summit

Investors Will Lead Private Discussions With Distinguished Hedge Fund Managers In An Elegant And Discreet Setting. Participation In This Exclusive Event Is By Invitation Only. Hedge Fund Managers And Qualified Investors Who May Wish To Participate In This Event Should Write . . .

Although the credit crisis has caused a massive melt down in the financial markets, there are still opportunities in several sectors. We will explore how investors and hedge funds alike are navigating these difficult waters. And we will try to identify what strategies will generate alpha during the next year.

'Identifying the Next Generation of Alpha', 10 December 2008

Decomposing stock returns

The investment strategy proposed is based on the following principles:

- The 'long' bias is optimized through a TAA process
- We smooth TAA performance with DJ EuroStoxx 50 Options
- We generate alphas through a sector rotation strategy
- We implement truncated return strategies eliminating the worst (and best) returns for the fund track record using options or sector indexes
- This research is supported by Eurex . . .
- Stock (excess) returns can be decomposed into a systematic and a specific component . . .
- There is little evidence of predictability in specific component (more noisy) in the absence of private information . . .

Daniel, Grinblatt, Titman and Wermers (*Journal of Finance*, 1997): 'We find no evidence that funds are successful style timers . . . Our application . . . suggests that, as a group, the funds showed some stock selection ability, but no discernable ability to time the different stock characteristics (e.g., buying high book-to-market stocks when those stocks have unusually high returns). We . . . find no convincing evidence of individual funds successfully timing the characteristics.'

- Stock picking is already challenger per say without adding the complexity of style timing . . .

  Tactical Style Allocation (TSA), a new form of market neutral strategy by Professor Noël Amenc, Edhec Risk and Asset Management Research Centre

The lag value of the term spread

Economic intuition about the differential small versus large cap and the lagged return on large cap stocks . . .

- This is consistent with the lead–lag pattern uncovered by Lo and MacKinlay (1990) . . . Economic intuition about the differential small versus large cap and the lagged value of the term spread

- A steeply upward (downward) slopping yield curve signals expectations of rising (decreasing) short-term interest rates in the future

- Increases in interest rates have a negative impact on large cap stock returns, and a subsequent similar impact on small cap stock return through the lead-lag effect

Amenc

Upward slopping yield curve

- When the term spread is low (downward or slightly upward slopping yield curve), S&P 500 outperforms S&P 600 SC one month lather by an annualized 7.70% on average

- When the term spread is high (steeply upward slopping yield curve), S&P 500 underperforms S&) 600 SC one month later by an annualized 6.74% on average.

Amenc

Future correlates with volatility

The predictability of future results shows a strong correlation with the volatility of each strategy. Future performance of strategies with high volatility is far less predictable than future performance from strategies experiencing low or moderate volatility.

www.magnum.com

Morningstar box equates to drift

. . . while there's some utility in evaluating style drift, the key thing for investors to focus on is strategy drift. As such, investors should not automatically assume that a shift in the Morningstar style box automatically equates to style drift.

Kupal Kapoor

Correction for heteroskedasticity

- Tests for detecting heteroskedasticity: White (1980)
- The correction for heteroskedasticity involves weighted (or generalized) least squares

Amenc

Chow test

Checking the robustness of the model through time

- Models are dynamically calibrated
- We use Chow test as a parameter stability test
- When appropriate, we use Kalman filter analysis, where priors on model parameters are recursively updated in reaction to new information
- Conditional models are attractive but they involve additional parameters and often result in lower out-of-sample performance

Amenc

Mistakes were made

AIG (AIG: down $0.31 to $60.27, Research, Estimates) developed and marketed a 'non-traditional' insurance product for Brightpoint that made the company appear that it was paying premiums in return for the assumption of risk by AIG.

However, Brightpoint, which was hit with a $450,000 civil penalty, used the product to deposit cash with AIG and the funds were later returned to the company, the SEC said in a written statement. As a result of the transaction, the AIG product helped Brightpoint conceal losses of $11.9 million in 1998, and its full-year net-income before taxes was overstated by 61 percent that year, according to the SEC. 'This transaction was simply a "round-trip" of cash from Brightpoint to AIG and back to Brightpoint,' said Wayne Carlin, Regional Director of the Commission's Northeast Regional Office. 'By disguising the money as "insurance," AIG enabled Brightpoint to spread over several years a loss that should have been recognized immediately.' In a written statement Thursday, AIG acknowledged that 'mistakes were made with the underwriting of this policy.'

www.money.cnn.com, 11 September 2003

Lagged variable impact style differential – a difficult art

We have just seen a series of examples illustrating that both contemporaneous and lagged economic and financial variables had an impact on style differentials (growth – value, large – small cap).

Forecasting economic variables is a difficult art, with the failures often leading to all systematic tactical allocation processes being abandoned.

Two ways of considering tactical style allocation:

- Forecasting returns is based on forecasting the values of economic variables (scenarios on the contemporaneous variables)

- Forecasting returns is based on anticipating market reactions to known economic variables (econometric model with lagged variables)

Amenc

Offset long-only portfolios

Short Selling: Sells securities short in anticipation of being able to rebuy them at a future date at a lower price due to the manager's assessment of the overvaluation of the securities, or the market, or in anticipation of earnings disappointments often due to accounting irregularities, new competition, change of management, etc. Often used as a hedge to offset long-only portfolios and by those who feel the market is approaching a bearish cycle. High risk. Expected Volatility: Very High.

www.magnum.com

Hedge fund parlance

The business of risk arbitrage has a more long-term view that is called 'market neutral' in hedge-fund parlance because the investment horizons for M&A bets are the months, or years, between the first announcement of a deal and the final closing. And when the broader market machinations did factor into an arbitragers decisions, it was because various deals depended on financing, which in turn could depend on stock movements . . .

www.blogs.wsj.com/deals

Alerting exit criteria

There is no certainty of outcomes, but if one follows criteria that have a statistically defined probability of occurring, then when those criteria mesh to create an alert they learn to trust the alert knowing that if they are right, they will enjoy the benefits and if they are wrong they will cut their losses when their exit criteria is alerted.

From *Sharesender*, an investment company's media release

Readers for whom the parlance of the free market is proving unbearable should alert their exit criteria and proceed to Government on page 213.

Modeling sensitivity

We will be modeling various sensitivities [to?] determine the best strategies to optimize our strong originations forecast and manage asset growth and capital. In addition, we will prioritize the launch of new growth initiatives, as well as the timing of these investments in comparison to the revenue projections.

In a corporate memo from a US-owned Canadian company

One helluva real-time customizable platform

Hedge funds that treat forex options as an asset class can view relative value and spread data on these instruments. Corporates can monitor and chart spot forex rates or price options or revalue a portfolio of options. Emerging-market investors can plot emerging-market government bonds against corporates. There really is no limit to the types of data that can be analysed here. Other banks may have superior individual analytics tools, but none of them can combine them all into one real-time customizable platform.

www.euromoney.com

Romantic step investments

Storm even coined a new and unusual term for the growth of its business, to reflect the role debt played in growing client portfolios.

Unlike other wealth management companies, which record 'funds under management' or something similar, Storm measured 'funds and liabilities under advice', and between 2004 and the start of 2008 the so-called 'funds and liabilities under advice' grew from $1.4 billion to just over $6 billion – annual growth of 45 per cent . . .

'People were romanced by all the hype in the way these products were sold,' [Saskia ten Dam, a financial counsellor with the Townsville Community Legal Service] said . . .

In Storm-speak, additional investments were called 'step investments' and, regardless of whether the market was rising or falling, Storm encouraged clients to use debt to bulk up their portfolio.

By early 2008, fees generated by step investments accounted for more than 60 per cent of Storm's income.

The Age, 17 January 2009

Very Darwinian model

'Looking forward, we have to conclude that the hedge fund model will remain quite powerful, in my view. It has a very low leverage,' he added . . . It's a very Darwinian model where only the best survive.

Reuters, 23 February 2009

Very Darwinian people

'These people [hedge funds] will possibly prove to be more resilient than people thought,' said Antonio

Borges, chairman of the Hedge Funds Standards
Board.

Reuters, 23 February 2009

Highly sophisticated they are

SPIEGEL: Mr Paulson, the global economy is shaky:
China is flooding the world with cheap products. The
Americans have to finance their spending sprees with
loans, and worried Germans are saving every euro they
can. How long can this last?

HENRY PAULSON (CEO of Goldman Sachs, on the eve
of his becoming US Treasury Secretary): I don't share
your pessimism . . .

SPIEGEL: One other scenario is conceivable: The dollar
crashes, interest rates take off, oil prices climb, the
US real-estate bubble bursts, the American consumer
stops spending – and the global economy collapses.

HENRY PAULSON: The risk I worry about the least right
now is a dramatic drop in the dollar. And I don't
believe there is a general housing bubble. There
might be anomalies in certain regions but I don't see
a real estate bubble across the US. What I am really
concerned about is energy prices. A cold winter in the
US could affect growth and the behavior of consumers.
But, having said that, who would have thought two
years ago that the US, Japan, China and parts of
Europe would be doing as well as they are right now?
From my perspective the glass is half full rather than
half empty.

SPIEGEL: Don't hedge funds have far too much power?

HENRY PAULSON: Most hedge funds are run by highly
sophisticated investors and many of them are long-
term investors. They provide liquidity and also play

an important role in addressing corporate governance issues. From my perspective, it is a mistake to demonize them . . .

SPIEGEL: . . . risky instruments such as hedge funds and credit derivatives are barely regulated. Why?

HENRY PAULSON: The fact is these instruments have grown extremely quickly and regulatory bodies have relatively little experience of how to deal with them. But it is inaccurate to say that there is no regulation and there are also a lot of discussions going on between the relevant authorities and market participants. I am sure that much thought and action will take place in this area, particularly within the industry, and all parties involved need to do their part.

SPIEGEL: The crash of the LTCM fund brought the world economy to the brink of disaster in 1998. Is a similar crisis around the corner now?

HENRY PAULSON: Since then we have not seen a comparable financial shock globally. We have gone through the Internet bubble and September 11. There have been wars and spectacular corporate failures. Nevertheless, there has been no genuine crisis in the financial markets so far . . .

SPIEGEL: But voluntary commitments don't help. We would feel more secure if there were some form of government regulation.

HENRY PAULSON: SEC registration of hedge funds is a positive step and certainly helps create greater transparency. But I believe it would be a mistake to deprive hedge funds of their flexibility. They make a major contribution to market efficiency.

SPIEGEL: The world is more tightly networked today than ever before. The next crash would be much more dramatic . . .

HENRY PAULSON: Just think of the collapses of Enron and WorldCom. They had an enormous impact on the business community and on the rules and regulations for joint stock corporations. But the financial markets absorbed the shocks reasonably well. One reason for this is the development of relatively new financial instruments, such as credit derivatives, that have made it possible to manage risks better. That has been a major breakthrough.

Spiegel Online, 31 May 2006

Compensation

In its Latin origins this means to weigh things, to balance one against the other, to make equivalent in value, to requite suitably. Anyone speak Latin? 'The length of the night and the dews thereof do compensate the heat of the day' – maybe, but these guys work the length of the day *and* the night and wouldn't know the dews if they fell on them. The poor souls, for their companies they have relinquished the experience of Nature.

Theirs is a kind of *buy-in* that can't be *balanced* against the wages of the window-cleaners or any of those ant-like things shuffling through their days down on the street – and worth, as the market's unseen hand affirms, one three-hundred-and-forty-fourth of the CEO at Merrill Lynch. It's not as if *society* got their buy-in, is it? It wasn't for *society* that they worked 24/7. These guys don't even believe in society. They never heard of it. Did they do their MBAs to learn about society? But now this 'society', this chimera, lumbers from its hiding place bellowing about corporate thieves. So now 'society' says every common thief can call his loot *compensation*? The world's gone mad.

Compensation to drive the right behaviours

To facilitate the independent advice that Compensation Committees and management need in today's heavily scrutinized executive compensation climate, we offer a broad array of compensation and rewards services – ranging from total rewards strategy to competitive benchmarking to incentive plan design. We work with companies to ensure that their compensation programs drive the right behaviors, are competitively positioned, are compliant with technical and regulatory requirements, and support strategic business objectives.

www.jfreda.com

Not much money

'That is pretty draconian – $500,000 is not a lot of money, particularly if there is no bonus,' said James F. Reda, founder and managing director of James F. Reda & Associates, a compensation consulting firm . . . Mr Reda said only a handful of big companies pay chief executives and other senior executives $500,000 or less in total compensation.

The New York Times, 3 February 2009

Achieve your compensation strategy

Total Compensation Solutions

TCS is an independent human resources consulting firm dedicated to applied research and assisting clients achieve their strategic compensation objectives. Our approach to compensation and benefits issues is to utilize data to identify best practices in the marketplace. Specializing in: Executive Compensation, Salary Administration, Incentive

Compensation Planning, Sales Force Compensation, Survey Consulting, Board of Directors Compensation, and Executive Deferred Compensation.

www.total-comp.com

CEO's pay slashed to $25 million

Ford Motor Co President and CEO Alan Mulally received compensation valued at $US17.7 million ($A25.12 million) in 2008, down more than 22 per cent from the prior year, as the automaker struggles amid the worst US auto sales slump in 27 years, according to a federal regulatory filing published on Tuesday.

www.businessday.com.au

Certain nonprofit market factors

'There is no doubt that $1.1 million is a great deal of compensation,' Noren said. 'However, the board strongly believes that this was well earned.' . . . Gianelli defended their pay, saying the compensation was in line with industry standards and appropriately recognized talent. 'Certainly, we want the best people running our hospitals, and the compensation for the executives is determined by the boards of the hospitals,' she said. 'They base those decisions on the market and on their own internal compensation studies, on the hospitals' performance, and on other considerations, such as certain market factors.'

Asked if people might be shocked to see high levels of compensation paid by hospitals that with one exception . . . are technically nonprofit institutions, Gianelli cited what she said were the executives' wide range of responsibilities.

Journal Inquirer, 29 April 2009

Government

Once upon a time government bureaucrats spoke 'bureaucratese'. It was a confounding, irritating language, but at least it was amusing to other bureaucrats – and it did have recognisable roots in general English. The art is all but lost. Government departments are now run according to the same managerial principles as those that rule the private sector: they engage the same consultants, send their executives to the same courses, hold the same team-building exercises and employ similar principles of accounting. It was inevitable that they would also come to speak the same management language, and, in the manner of the recent convert, to speak it more extremely.

The people who write this way, or at least those who demand that they do, must have some aim in mind; something about the tone of it must please them. Probably it is the bloodlessness and the pretence of objectivity. There are a great many *frameworks*, *platforms* and *scaffoldings*; *objectives*, *outputs* and *inputs*; a lot of stuff that is *key*, *strategic* and *enhanced* and a lot of *underpinned vision*: as if every worker in a health department is never far from a dictionary of civil engineering.

The first thing to know about government agencies is that they seek *outcomes*. Policy, according to one government definition, 'is a mechanism for the translation of the priorities and values of the organisation into programs and practices to deliver outcomes'. The mistake is to imagine that the outcomes they seek must be for you. In fact, the outcomes

that government bureaucracies
and their ministers so much desire
are very often outcomes for those
bureaucracies and those ministers.

Tasmanian outcomes

> Target outcomes are expressed
> as a sentence in the past
> tense and usually start with
> a word ending in *ed*, such
> as improved, increased,
> enhanced or reduced.
> Framing target outcomes
> in this way makes it easier
> to determine their success
> measure.
>
> Tasmanian Government

A useful way to frame the objective is to answer the
question why are you doing the project? The result
is a one sentence statement, or series of statements,
starting with the word *To*.

Tasmanian Government

Outcomes are the benefits or other long-term changes
that are sought from undertaking the project. They are
achieved from the utilisation of the projects outputs.
Outcomes are linked with objectives, in that if the
outcomes are achieved then the projects objective(s)
have been met.

Tasmanian Government

Measurable benefits that are sought from undertaking
a project. Target Outcomes are achieved from the
utilisation of the outputs delivered by a project. Stated,

identified targets and measures are developed for gauging progress towards their achievements.

Tasmanian Government

Target Outcomes for a project are outcomes that have a measurable benefit and will be used to gauge the success of the project. Usually there will only be a small number of target outcomes for any project. Each measure will be linked to one or more target outcomes. At the end of the project the measures will help answer such questions as what have we achieved? and how do we know?

Tasmanian Government

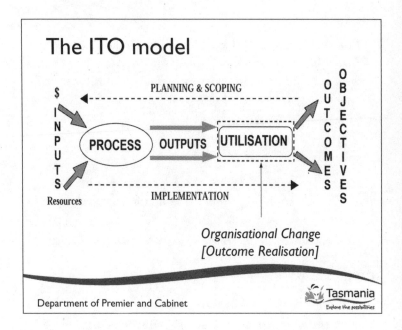

Gully eduction outcome

The city has just introduced an in-house sweeping service and is seeking someone with a current HR drivers licence who is experienced in sweeping services, including gully eduction.

The Times of Joondalup, Western Australia, 23 December 2008

At last – a strategic plan!

Stakeholder UpDate Two, August 2008. Our Vision is to improve the quality of life of all in Central Bedfordshire, and enhance the unique character of our communities and our environment. Moving forward! . . . We are now able to create a Strategic Plan based upon the agreed Vision, Values and Priorities.

Central Bedfordshire Council, United Kingdom

The delivering

The Delivering a Healthy WA Communication Style Guide has been developed to assist with integrating the visual identity into existing or new communication materials.

Western Australian Health Department

Absolutely key

We think it's absolutely key that we get the population of workers, students, residents and visitors up to a critical mass that's sustainable.

Michael Harbison, Lord Mayor of Adelaide, *Adelaide Advertiser*, 15 May 2006

ICBT

. . . intellectual capacity-building tour . . .

The head of the Finance Committee for the Auckland City Council describes his $30,000 trip to Europe, *New Zealand Herald*, 12 April 2006

Tasmanian objectives

A project objective is a statement of the overarching rationale for why the project is being conducted.

Tasmanian Government

Outcomes/benefits realisation satisfies business drivers

Whether the stakeholders are citizens, politicians, agency employees or other constituents, effective utilisation requires specific organisational change to satisfy the business drivers, thereby enabling the projects outcomes to be realised. The Tasmanian Government Project Management Guidelines refers to this stage of the project as outcome/benefits realisation.

Outcome Realisation and Organisational Change Management: the Tasmanian government approach

Tangible things

Outputs: tangible things projects create to achieve the Outcomes.

Project Closure: Acceptance of outputs by the business owner/s — plan well ahead.

- Disband Project Team
- Review
- Celebrate

Tasmanian Government

Outputs

Outputs

Outputs are the products, services, business or management practices that will be required (produced) to meet the identified outcomes/benefits. They may be new products or services, or fixed things called alterants. Outputs link with outcomes, in that the outputs are used by the projects customers to achieve the outcomes.

Outputs are usually expressed as nouns.

Tasmanian Government

Plan accordingly

Outcome realisation and project closure need to be planned accordingly, they are separate activities.

Tasmanian Government

Powerful aligned library

THE VISION OF CAIRNS LIBRARIES is to be a sustainable world class Library Service, recognised as an innovative, professional and powerful contributor to the quality of life and lifelong learning of the region, and a successful, effective and viable Business Branch of Cairns Regional Council aligned to the principles of Business Excellence.

Cairns Libraries

Key principles underpinning excellence

Noosa Council — innovative and effective leadership that facilitates preferred community outcomes.

Vision:

Noosa Shire is an inclusive community renowned for its creativity, innovation, vision and entrepreneurship where sustainability underpins excellence.

The key principles that underpin the vision are:

- Social cohesion and community well-being;
- Strong sustainable economy;
- Environmental excellence and sustainability;

- Artistic and cultural diversity and excellence;

- A commitment to maintaining a sustainable population;

- Quality, innovative and reliable infrastructure; and

- Maintaining the 'Noosa Style'.

Noosa, Queensland

Strategies targeting manifestations

Hi everyone,

My concern at this point in time is about the process rather than the alignment of risk manifestation to broader risk categories – logic or otherwise noting I too share concerns about the logic of some of the recent 'grouping' decisions of specific manifestations to broader risks. Notwithstanding, the grouping principle is sound in my view providing the broader risk categories are well constructed (from a logical and hierarchical perspective) and clearly articulate the risks to our objectives.

I also share concerns about not quantifying the manifestation of the risk itself through a separate risk assessment process and just showing it's impact to the existing broader risk in existing documents. It's too veiled and veneer in approach and more importantly, does not lend itself to measuring the compliance effectiveness of strategies targeting manifestations.

Logic dictates if we are adding a manifestation then there is a reason for it – normally made transparent through a risk assessment process that identifies threats, impact areas, and control mechanisms that are in place to enable us to measure likelihood and consequences. In this regard the risk assessment is a natural precursor to the processes I mentioned below and not intended to bypass the risk assessment process altogether. Note the process below is specifically aimed at updating and presenting high level documents for both information and endorsement which doesn't necessarily preclude a specific risk assessment per se. Admittedly, it may give that impression.

An email from someone at the Australian Taxation Office; subject: Treatment strategies for manifestations of category risks

Unlikely commitment

Achieving global commitment to emissions reductions of this order appears unlikely in the next commitment period.

Commonwealth Government Emissions Trading White Paper

Drill down, set up, roll out – inject!

You'll drill down into how to set up and roll out a performance improvement framework in your organization . . . You'll benchmark how to integrate your disparate systems into one streamlined performance management framework and how to inject greater customer centricity into your service delivery initiatives.

Performance Improvement Frameworks for Government Service Delivery Conference

Iteration beyond the fruit

Partnering for Profit: Creating Value from Internal Business Alignment

Recently, organizations have focused more intently on locking the next iteration of procurement value, beyond the 'low-hanging' fruit. Best-in-class organizations are migrating towards a more strategic mindset by emphasizing deep partnerships with internal customers and suppliers.

From the Good Procurement Guide: Launch & Creating Value from Internal Business Alignment Workshop, run by the Government Reform Commission

Window on to the same page

I believe we have a great window of opportunity over the next few years to get all Australians government on the same page . . . Three years on that window of opportunity is still open and the mood far more cooperative – but the need for decisive action is acute.

John Brumby, VECCI address, 27 November 08

In terms of a blowtorch

The commencement date should occur in the context of having firm commitments from the rest of the world in terms of what they are going to do . . . it should occur in an environment where the blowtorch has been applied to the major emitters throughout the world and we have a commitment from them in terms of the action that they will actually undertake.

Opposition leader Brendan Nelson, agreeing with his shadow minister Greg Hunt that the opposition's commitment to 2012 for the start of an Emissions Trading Scheme is 'rock-solid'

Communicating to the public information

Entitled 'An Australian Consumer Law: better regulation – confident consumers', this paper communicates to the public information about COAG's agreed consumer reforms and the process for developing the national law. It also invites the public to submit their views on the process, so that we can move forward with direct engagement from all relevant stakeholders.

Chris Bowen, Assistant Treasurer and Minister for Competition Policy and Consumer Affairs, 17 February 2009

Avenues for multi-disciplinary solutions

The Fund seeks to showcase smarter ways to save water through innovative solutions in order to empower the community and business sectors to respond to the call to save water. It provides avenues for multi-disciplinary solutions to be explored as the solutions of the future may lie in the engineering or science disciplines or in modification to social norms and behaviours or a combination of all!

The Smart Water Fund

What the framework means

The committee recommends that the Scottish Government should publish, in future, an assessment matrix of candidate national developments against the national development criteria. There is still room for improvement, particularly in the use of language, which will help improve understanding and potentially also improve public engagement if there is a greater understanding of what the framework actually means to individuals.

Report of Scottish Government committee that also recommends that ministers use jargon-free language. BBC News

Thought leaders using a world café structure

At the very core of the learning design that underpins the program is the acknowledgement and belief that the Symposium will bring a group of capable, knowledgeable, experienced and passionate leaders and practitioners from Local Government across NSW. It utilises adult learning principles and positions delegates as active participants there to share, experience and reflect – not just to learn.

Initially, keynotes by thought leaders will set the problem context for the day and this will then be questioned and further clarified by high level panellists. A facilitator will draw questions from the delegates and build a discussion around key themes.

Delegates will then engage with each other through deliberative dialogues using a World Café structure to explore the implications and priorities for Councils given the challenges outlined in the prior session. Through table facilitators, the deliberative dialogues will generate a series of outputs that document the key priorities and directions for integrating sustainability.

Delegates will be able to select a concurrent skills workshop that explores specific tools and processes for integrated sustainability. Delegates will be engaged in small group workshops to consider how each tool will support and potentially expand their capacity to develop an integrated approach.

NSW Department of Environment and Climate Change

Deliverable platform

Another key deliverable in the establishment of the Smart Water Fund was to provide a platform for specific research and development into the key challenges facing the Victorian water industry.

The Smart Water Fund

Enhanced platform

The new catalogue is part of an enhanced platform to access the Library's unrivalled digital resources in this collection. With this robust platform, we will be able to increase the rate of digitisation of material and records . . .

State Library of New South Wales

Positioning the umbrella

The aim of the Umbrella Policy is to define the key goals and objectives that drive the arts and cultural development activity of the Directorate . . . Positioning of the Umbrella Policy Framework (vision, outcomes etc. in a flow chart)

Western Australian Government

Under the umbrella

IBSA is embarking on a twofold project with XXXX Management which, in collaboration with CITT, will run in parallel with the current ICT02 Project and fall under the umbrella of the existing NPRG.

Correspondence from IBSA to state training authorities

People up the pipeline

SOURCING – BUILDING TALENT PIPELINES AND SUPPLY CHAINS – A PEOPLE STRATEGY PROJECT

. . . the department has embarked on a number of key projects that collectively are aimed at tackling these issues. More specifically, one of the projects relates to assessing and subsequently implementing several candidate sourcing strategies. The project is referred to as 'Sourcing – Building talent pipelines and supply chains' and the first phase involves the engagement of an external provider who will assist the department in researching and identifying best practice sourcing strategies that are appropriate and adaptable for the

Department of Human Services. The department recognises the need to be more proactive, innovative and less administrative in the way it attracts recruits and retains employees across all levels and role types.

An email to government employees

Do you *understand*?

. . . learning-based change for environmental sustainability [which] is the development of knowledge, skills, values, attitudes and aspirations leading to changed behaviour in support of environment sustainability.

Learning to Live Sustainably, Department of Sustainability and Environment, Victoria

Engaged in sharp focused consultation

Living its charter to build capability and professionalism within the business community, IBSA actively engages in sharp-focused consultation with industry to gather market intelligence on trends and skill needs enabling it to develop training products for the vocational education and training (VET) sector designed to foster innovation in thinking and practice.

Innovation and Business Skills Australia

Heterodyning outputs

The result appears to be a fragmented and uncoordinated approach that would efficiently be implemented by the heterodyning of these areas' outputs through a strategic planning document.

From a classified document

Empowering all three both

By empowering both industrial water users, community organisations and individuals to develop their own innovative water conservation solutions, the Smart Water Fund is creating water conservation ambassadors at all levels of society.

The Smart Water Fund

Incentive for modal share

QR recognises that the effective management of the national rail asset is critical to provide an incentive for modal share consistent with optimised allocative efficiencies.

Queensland Rail submission to productivity commission

Homeland security landscape

The NIMS is a dynamic system, and the doctrine as well as the implementation requirements will continue to evolve as our prevention, preparedness, response, and recovery capabilities improve and our homeland security landscape changes. It is critical NIMS baseline training becomes an integral part of the organization's training program. Organizational changes as a result of new hires, promotions or mission changes amplify this training requirement.

FEMA, United States

Non-identity card

It's not an identity card . . . it's an access card that's used to authenticate identity.

A spokeswoman for Human Services Minister Joe Hockey

Non-electric energised courtesy fence

I asked (the Deputy Secretary of the Department
of Immigration) a question about a fence which
surrounds the Baxter Detention Centre. The fence is
described on a plan of Baxter as a 'courtesy fence'.
I suggested that it was in fact an electric fence. 'No,'
she insisted, 'it is not an electric fence. It is an
energized fence.' A 9000-volt energized fence.

From a speech by Julian Burnside given on I March 2005

Brochure for those who can't read

If you cannot read, this brochure tells you where to get
lessons.

Centrelink leaflet on multi-cultural services

Missing factual matrix

If accepted, (and we note that the factual matrix on
which this hypothesis rests is not made out), it would
not help . . .

Tasmanian Anti Discrimination Tribunal

The tool's perspective

This is a support role that provides change leadership
cross-functionally within a project management
context. It leads the development and provision of
tools, advice, support, methodologies and frameworks
for change professionals across the Department
of Housing. It operates in a context of consistent
change either from a policy, practice or support tool
perspective. This change is generated by business need
to meet the strategic directions that the business has
undertaken. The change may be generated corporately
or from a divisional perspective.

Project Change Manager – a position description at the NSW Department of Housing

Transformation program

To resolve this our Transformation Program will . . . lift capacity and capability by implementing team structures, coaching, succession planning and a new performance management framework . . .

From the Transformation Stakeholder Document Letter, CEO Standards Australia

The commitments

The government is committed to active engagement with the social partners on the future of the commercial semi-state sector on the basis of the government's commitment to its role in providing services of world-class quality at a competitive price to the consumer with a viable long-term future for individual companies based on the most appropriate form of ownership or structure for its particular needs.

The Irish Government's 'Towards 2016: Ten-year Framework Social Partnership Agreement 2006–2015'

End to end

The Respondent Is To Provide Strategic Advice On The Integration And Co-Ordination Of The Various Disciplines Utilised In Reviewing And Structuring The Ongoing Reforms In Defence's Procurement And Contracting Lifecycle In Order To Provide 'End To End' Overview And Consistency And Assist In The Development And Implementation Of Such Reforms Including . . .

Skill SET: Provision of Strategic Advisers, Australian Defence Department

Vrigorous KRAs

Our KRAs need to be vigorous and rigorous.

Victorian Department of Sustainability and Environment

Assistance

The Corporate Services Reform Unit works with agencies to assist their delivery of sustainable service improvement and cost reduction through an integrated program of shared learning, common frameworks, capability enhancement, benchmarking, on-site assistance with process streamlining, and technology lifecycle management.

Public Administration Today, July–October 2005

Valued parking inspector customer

Customer Service Officer.

Seen on yellow safety vest worn by a parking inspector

Encompass quality/process output – and pinpoint

We have a metrics portfolio that extends beyond efficiency metrics to encompass quality/process output measures and pinpoint areas for improvement.

From a draft document about managing the Department for Victorian Communities' recruitment processes

Covert optics

Fraud that is sophisticated and elaborate sometimes requires non-traditional evidence-gathering tools, such as covert optical surveillance.

Centrelink General Manager talking about hiring private eyes to catch welfare cheats

Good better best (practice)

. . . we looked inside our organisation and found that some people were doing good best practice . . .

NSW Roads & Traffic Authority presenter at a seminar called 'Attracting, retaining and sustaining high performance employees' – first in a line collectively called 'The Masterclass Series'

But how will they align them?

In moving forward, COAG has tasked officials with completing specific reform proposals for its consideration at its next meeting. These reform proposals will include, as necessary and appropriate, agreed policy directions, outcomes and commitments, multilateral and jurisdictional specific actions, progress measures and milestones.

The Council of Australian Governments

Indecapitation

What we train our officers to do is what we call immediate incapacitation . . . Which is aiming for the head. I understand why it is that people say that's a shoot to kill policy but it is not a shoot to kill policy . . . They shoot to incapacitate.

Assistant Commissioner Steve House, London Metropolitan Police, 8 March 2006

Medical termination issue

Defence has been working very hard to resolve what is a medical termination issue. Late last year, following receipt of specialist report which supported the upgrade of her medical status, Lieutenant Commander Fahy became fully employable, and Navy has attempted to generate, with her, a mutually agreed posting plan.

Andrew Nikolic, ABC Radio 16 May 2006

A set or outcomes

I think we've moved on from that, the travelling public and the workforce accept that it's a new paradigm, a new set of relationships that deliver a better set of outcomes.

Victoria's Transport Minister, Peter Batchelor, on why the government should take back the transport system after a report found that its sale had cost $1.2 billion in public subsidies

Strategy to underpin target

We've started off at a very conceptual level with our target. We're now working on the strategy that will underpin those targets . . .

Director of SA Council of Social Services

Budget to underpin strategy

The budget is the financial plan of the authority and as such will underpin the delivery of the Community Strategy Priorities over the medium term and reflect the council's assessment of service priorities. The budget is at the heart of the Community Strategy Priorities . . .

Slough Borough Council, Report to Cabinet, 24 September 2008

Medium Strategy to underpin plan

A golden thread links the Corporate Plan, which is under pinned by the Medium Term Strategy to Directorate Service Plans and individual staff appraisals . . .

Slough Borough Council

Clear outcomes with actions to underpin high level vision

The Strategy will set out a high level vision that will be underpinned by clear outcomes with actions, target dates and performance measures. The Strategy will align relevant policies and initiatives to help improve integration across governments and in related policy areas.

Australian Government, Developing a National Disability Strategy

Science . . .

The Cynefin framework . . . has been recognized by several commentators as one of the first practical applications of complexity theory to management science and builds on earlier pioneering work in Knowledge Management.

Director of the Cynefin Centre for Organizational Complexity, Knowledge & Continuous Improvement lunch, run by the Victorian Public Service Continuous Improvement Network

More science . . .

Earlier this week the Safety Incident Management System (SIMS) was upgraded. A notification system which escalates open (not closed) incidents has been added. This advises employees, supervisors and managers that a hazard or incident entered in SIMS requires further action. The notification system will ensure that hazards and incidents are speedily and effectively managed.

From a 'Director of People & Culture'

And more still . . .

Recognising that a national framework for comparison of water accounting systems can encourage continuous improvement leading to adoption of best practice . . .

The National Water Initiative

And yet more

Delivering transformational tools and methods of analysis to decision makers through productive partnerships and research excellence.

CSIRO's Division of Mathematical and Information Sciences bookmark

The miracle of the knowledge desk

The Centrelink contact point for statistics, previously known as the Centrelink Knowledge Desk is now known as the Business Intelligence Frontdoor.

Centrelink

Impacts on stakeholders

While many stakeholders and their interests are self-evident in the impacts noted for issues, areas and industries, we have conducted a brief overview of all stakeholders to ensure that none that might experience significant positive or negative impacts resulting from increased environmental flows escape attention.

From 'Scoping Study for Social Impact Assessment of Possible Increases in Environmental Flow Allocations to the River Murray System', prepared for Murray-Darling Basin Commission by Hassall and Associates and Helen Ross, University of Queensland, June 2003

Everyone talking about transparency

It's a kind of ring-fencing between the retail and wholesale divisions of Telstra so that there's much greater transparency. That is what everyone who's talking about breaking Telstra up is really talking about. They're talking about transparency.

Communications Minister Senator Helen Coonan, *Sunday*, Channel Nine, 13 March 2005

SIPs outlets

Stocked Impoundment Permits (SIPs) are for sale at various outlets.

Fishing licences sold by the Queensland Government

Customer service delivery conducive

In order to better prepare ourselves for coming systems changes, office refurbishment, as well as providing a more supportive & Customer service delivery conducive working environment, the CSBC have realigned some work structures & flows in order to improve how we do business.

Australian Electoral Commission email, January 2005

Outcomes of impact

The CSIRO Strategic Plan for 2003–2007 outlines our organisation's goals, strategic objectives, targets and performance metrics for the next four year period. Focussing on delivery and execution, it is the second in a series of strategic plans that are guiding our vision for the future . . . Our goals will be achieved by our unremitting excellence in research, focussing on key national challenges and embracing global opportunities. We will deliver outcomes of true value and impact, unleashing our creative abilities. We are building a research enterprise with truly global connections and stature.

CSIRO

Re-engineered transparency frameworks

Issues of legislative reform, best practice corporate governance and the re-engineering of accountability and transparency frameworks for improved service delivery, confront all departments, regardless of their individual strategies.

A conference on Accountability, Transparency and Performance in the Public Sector

Removal operation

Another spokesman for the Department, Mr Andrew Gavin, did confirm that a 'removal operation' had taken place on 13 December last year . . . and was able to clarify that a removal operation is different from a deportation, which is what happens when Australia deports criminals, but refused to discuss any particulars or the details of the operation.

www.newmatilda.com, January 2005

The face of the man in the middle was partly covered by shiny black bands of gaffer tape that had been wound tightly around his head. His hair was sticking out in all directions and he was in chains. The gaffer tape covered the lower half of his face to his chin and pulled so tightly that the flesh around his cheeks was distorted. His nose was cramped leaving only a small amount of breathing room.

Sonia Chirgwin describing the 'removal operation' she saw on a Thai International Flight

EA2000APM for CWP cases

1. Key points

- Participation Reports should usually be submitted within 2 (& no later than 5) working days;

- complete Participation Reports in EA3000 CWC for WfD & EA2000APM for CWP cases;

- since 6 December 2004 Centrelink can make appointments into available IBTH sessions for participants who have been PR'd;

- therefore, CWCs are no longer required to make 'dummy' appointments for any PRs;

- when booking an appointment Centrelink will
  only see the 1st available IBTH session unless this
  is unsuitable & then other immediately available
  options will be shown.

  Centrelink

Relevant person (wildlife)

(2) in this section — 'relevant person', for a person,
means a person who would be a relevant person for
the person if the person were granted a commercial
wildlife licence under this chapter.

Nature Conservation Regulation 1994 – 182 Additional restriction for licence for
reptiles

Professional person (police)

We are committed to the ongoing professionalisation
of our profession, believing this to be the best way of
providing a strong policing service.

New South Wales Police Commissioner

Giving meaning to the framework

The purpose of the State Sustainability Strategy is to
illustrate how the State government will respond to
the sustainability agenda by adopting the sustainability
framework and highlighting actions across government
that give meaning to the framework. By focusing the
Strategy on agency activity, the State government
is demonstrating its important leadership role in
supporting the transition to a sustainable future.

The Western Australia State Sustainability Strategy

What about long-term announceables?

. . . but perhaps one of the mistakes of the past is to go

for shorter-term announceables, rather than long-term improvements.

Amanda Vanstone, *The Age*, 4 December 2004

Pull through

Communication must be open and honest. Tell it as it is. Stick to the facts and use high value information that will be 'pulled through' networks . . . Surveys conducted of body text indicate that 'every' reader would prefer the text to be printed in black — it aids concentration and comprehension.

Communications Principles, Internal Communications unit of the Communications and Stakeholder Relations division of the Victorian Department of Sustainability & Environment

Illegal product

. . . the vehicle was surveilled to an intersection where the product was seized.

Queensland police officer, ABC radio news, 19 November, 2004. The 'product' was ecstasy.

Non-monetary recognition opportunity

. . . be surprised and motivated by the strategic focus for a range of non-monetary recognition opportunities for the public and private sectors to enhance morale and productivity.

Recognition & Reward workshop for Queensland Government employees

Clarifying the objectives

Hi all —

I refer to a recent email on the above from [name 1] and a follow up response from [name 2] in relation to the seeking of details of the regional manager organisational arrangements for 05/06.

From discussions with [name 3], [name 4], etc I understand that you have recently met on this issue and general agreement was reached on the roles and responsibilities of the various regional management team members. I also understand that similar info has also been provided to HR in terms of formalising the regional management rearrangements.

I am currently seeking to obtain copies of the info discussed at the SDB meeting and that provided to HR to assess its worth in this exercise, however, in talking further with the Managers Bus Serv's this morning, it is apparent that the level of discussion to date has been re the roles and responsibilities at the regional manager level rather than at levels below these positions which defines the complete regional org structure and which in turn is used to create the new WBSE's.

As a consequence, the MBS's have taken on board the action to raise this issue with each of yourselves with a view to developing the necessary info relevant to your region. Given the general higher level agreement (with some minor exceptions . . .?) previously reached by yourselves, it is expected that such an exercise will result in a fair degree of consistency across the regions. Once this information is provided and aligned with deliverables and activities, FAM will create the new WBSE's, circulate them to the regions for review and the undertaking of the mapping exercise to align the old codes with the new.

I am forwarding this email in an attempt to clarify the need and the objectives of the request and to flag with yourselves that the MBS's will be raising this issue with you prior to the next SDB meeting where any further discussions and considerations can occur.

From the Queensland public service

Jargon-free jargon

This guide is part of the reputation management and external communications strategy approved by the executive.

Islington Council Style Guide to discourage the use of 'waffle and council speak'

It's not the destination but the improvement journey

The improvement journey continues in the pursuit of sustainable infrastructure to meet identified community service priorities.

2009 National Local Government Asset Management and Public Works Engineering Conference

To serve the customer, get the asset to perform?

. . . To truly achieve financial sustainability and deliver services to the expectations of the customer, Asset Managers must understand the service, the service levels required to meet the expectations of the customer and the demand on the service. By understanding this, the Asset Manager can truly determine the financial needs required for the asset to perform so that the service outcomes can be sustained for the life of the service . . .

2009 National Local Government Asset Management and Public Works Engineering Conference Australia

Making progress in testing theory

. . . In local government, the theory of asset management is often challenged by a number of factors including Council decisions, staff stress due to workload, and resource issues. Ngaire will explain her strategies for making progress in this environment . . .

2009 National Local Government Asset Management and Public Works Engineering Conference Australia

Bend straightening to be reviewed

My highways experts have looked at this draft as it relates to Titnore Lane, and have advised me that we are able to review the need, at this time, to require the developers to carry out bend straightening.

Councillor Lt Col Tex Pemberton, West Sussex

Unachievable budget for well being directorate event

5. 26 The pressures across the Central budgets have increased through an additional fall of £200k in income from local land charges (with the continuation of impact from the property market during the current economic climate) and also through the loss from the music event. It is anticipated these additional pressures will be contained by the year end. BPR savings that were built into the budgets for the Customer Service Centre in the Community and Well Being Directorate have now been adjusted as they were un-achievable.

Slough Borough Council

Understanding performance optimising triggers and pressing appropriate buttons in a timely fashion

High Performance Living is about understanding all your own triggers, and knowing which button to press at what time to optimise personal performance. Learn more about this process that scientifically increases performance by removing performance inhibitors and creating specific individual solutions. These solutions are then implemented to enhance performance on individual, management and organisational levels, as well as at home.

From a local government email listing training programs for staff, circulated by the human resources team

The outcomes of people

This new role will support delivery of genuine transformation of Adult Social Care in the East of England and also Local Authorities to develop innovative approaches tailored to local circumstances within the broad context of Putting People First. You will need to have a strategic overview about the future of social care and health in the context of Comprehensive Area Assessment – focussing on improving the outcomes of people. You will work closely with a broad range of stakeholders, senior Social Care and Health colleagues, elected Members, service users, carers, and other partners. The role is accountable to the Joint Improvement Partnership and links to ADASS and DH in the region and nationally . . .

Transforming Adult Social Care, Programme Director for Thurrock Council

Violent Crime Strategies with significant budget

Violent Crime Prevention Manager for Hackney council (£42,000)?

This important and high profile role will require coordinating partnership work to reduce violent crime, including violent extremism. Innovative in your approach, you will lead on the implementation of violent crime strategies and local action plans, ensuring key partners' involvement and commitment, while directly managing up to four officers and taking charge of a significant budget. Your proven track record in the community safety field will be complemented by in-depth knowledge of national legislation, strategies and guidelines in the areas of violent crime and preventing violent extremism. Skilled in developing strategies, analysing data and managing performance, you will have the ability to develop creative service solutions. A degree or equivalent experience will be essential.

www.telegraph.co.uk

Robust past with quokka

I'm not being backward in saying that I'm not a perfect individual and you know I've had a robust past and there may be elements of that that have proved offensive to people . . . Members of the press have in passing mentioned the word quokka and suggested to me that something inappropriate in the past may have happened . . . I don't shy away away from that at all, but I'm not aware that I've caused any offence to a quokka.

Troy Buswell, leader of the West Australian opposition, 14 May 2008

In terms of the shorter term in the term of the term of the Government

TONY JONES: You would want it resolved in this term of government, very briefly?

MARK VAILE: It's been the stated objective of the Government we do need to resolve it in this term of the Government. In fact, we may want to resolve it in the shorter term, but that's the process we'll embark upon in the shorter term in terms of what we need to do and if that reasonably fits into a pattern that will deliver us into a position of making that final decision.

Lateline, ABC TV, 23 June 2005

In terms of meat

I would say, just bear in mind the extensive access that New Zealand has into the European market – both in terms of dairy products, in terms of sheep meat or red

meats generally – compared to Australia. I mean we get
18,650 tons of sheep meat into the European Union.
The New Zealanders get hundreds of thousands – I
don't know the exact – they get hundreds of thousands
of sheep meat into the European Union. They get
massive access in terms of dairy products that we
basically get none.

Mark Vaile

Revitalised, internationally competitive, national, professional, integrated music

I appreciate your interest in the issue of elite
level classical music training in Australia and
wish to provide you with an update regarding the
Government's ongoing support for our most talented
classical musicians.

On 18 November 2008 I announced that
Australian Government funding of up to $2.5
million annually will be provided for a revitalised
elite level classical music performance and
training centre operating in conjunction with the
University of Melbourne's Faculty of the VCA and
Music . . .

If Australia is to remain internationally
competitive a strong multi-disciplinary and
comprehensive program is needed, linked to
an academic environment and integrated into
a professional arts precinct. Accordingly, the
University has appointed a Planning Advisory Board
comprised of leading international authorities on
elite music training to develop a truly world class
training program . . .

To meet the professional requirements of
Australia's orchestras, the revitalised ANAM program
will, for the first time, offer a national professional

performance program across the full range of instruments . . .

Peter Garrett, Minister for Environment, Heritage and the Arts, in a letter on
2 December 2008 to 750 signatories to a petition protesting at the closure of the
Australian National Academy of Music

Front-ending the denecessary

As the Government targeted the anti-deficit declaration in Parliament, Mr Springborg yesterday talked of 'front-ending' public service jobs and not refilling those considered 'denecessary'.

The Courier-Mail, 4 December 2008. Mr Springborg was leader of the Queensland opposition.

Reverse engineering lever – quick!

There has to be a greater synergy between, let's call it our policy leadership in this, which has been focused so much, legitimately, on targets and global architecture, almost reverse-engineered back to the means by which you can quickly deliver outcomes, and on the demand side in our economy we're looking at potential advances in terms of 20 to 25% range if you do this across the board. It all takes cost, but let me tell you it's probably the quickest lever you can pull given the challenges we face.

Kevin Rudd, Prime Minister of Australia

Tough pension reform commitment

Living on the single age pension is very, very tough, which is why we are committed to its reform.

Kevin Rudd, Prime Minister of Australia

Initiatives that exemplify strategies that improve outcomes for the needy

These pilots will trial or expand initiatives that exemplify strategies to improve literacy and numeracy outcomes for those students most in need of support . . .

Media release from Prime Minister Kevin Rudd and Julia Gillard, Deputy Prime Minister and Minister for Education

The key logic of artforms

This conference is positioned at the very edge of the politics of difference . . . The Conference will move beyond the closure and limits of current definitions that continue to divide and separate, whilst engaging with the possibilities of new convergent positions and space of shared cultural experience and knowledge. Global multiculturalism is a key logic of the cultures of the future.

Res Artis Conference, 2004

More key

Artform directors will be expected to understand and communicate with organisations in their artform . . .They must certainly understand the objectives and strategies of key organisations, and must consider how they fit in to the broader artform picture . . . It is proposed that some of these officers will reside in the new Key Organisations section.

Australia Council letter

Extraordinarily riveting

The skills required to evaluate and effectively support arts organisations differ from those required to manage a reactive grants process for specific Projects. This has been recognised in initiatives to build strategic planning skills both in the Australia Council and in arts companies, and also in dedication of staff in certain artforms to the relationship with triennially-funded organisations.

Australia Council letter

What Louise is

Louise is a committed arts practitioner

From the programme of the 31st Annual Knox Art Show

Council for greater arts impact

The Australia Council has to drive improvements in the arts sector, by building the capabilities of artists and arts organisations . . . to ensure we are a catalyst for greater impact . . . by building a vital and more viable art sector, and ensuring that all Australians are engaged with and enriched by the arts . . .

Media Release, Australia Council, December 2004

New and better knowledge

Strategy

Work with Knowledge Partners, particularly in the museum sector, in research, scholarship, education and exhibition development to create new and better knowledge and practices.

Result

A cost-effective program to produce high quality products achieved through collaborations with Australian and international museums and institutions, and with Knowledge Partners in the precinct.

www.powerhousemuseum.com

Promises to be triumph

Platforms for Collaboration

Under the National Collaborative Research Infrastructure Strategy (NCRIS) (a programme that was announced by the Australian Government in 2004 as part of Backing Australia's Ability – Building our Future through Science and Innovation), the Platforms for Collaboration capability was formed.

www.unisa.edu.au

Key floor target gaps

Floor target action plans

To assist neighbourhood Renewal Fund Local Strategic Partnerships (LSPs) to prepare plans to accelerate progress on key floor targets where the gap between their performance and national floor targets is widest. The five step approach enables LSPs to identify what existing plans and activities will deliver and, where necessary, what additional actions are needed to narrow the gap between expected performance and the relevant target. The guidance has now been integrated into the LSP Delivery Toolkit as the methodology provides an approach that can be adopted by LSPs in developing all plans including Local Area Agreements.

'Middlesbrough team guides you through the jargon', www.gazettelive.co.uk, 27 May 2009

A range of foci

Knowledge Transfer Networks

They were born out of Innovation and Growth Teams, developed out of Faradays, and combinations of Faradays and as a result of the Technology Programme April 2004 Competition. These different beginnings have given rise to a range of foci and scope, and allowed the evaluation of several different models of activity.

www.berr.gov.uk

Coherent

They are an evolving part of the overall Government Strategy and the Technology Strategy Board has put in place a review of their goals and activities which reflect their growing importance and to ensure that we move towards a coherent and integrated use of KTNs to feed and drive the Collaborative Research & Development programme and other innovation interventions.

www.berr.gov.uk

Overarching strategy to drive up quality

An overarching national improvement strategy will drive up quality and performance underpinned by specific plans for strategically significant areas of activity, such as workforce and technology.

UK Department for Innovation, Universities and Skills 2008 Annual Report

Physical activity

The Physical Activity Grants program supports increased involvement in physical activity by groups currently under represented in physical activity participation.

Victorian Government

Education

'Without a gentle contempt for education, no man's education is complete,' G. K. Chesterson said: but this is taking contempt too far. Says the NSW Board of Studies: 'Outcomes: The outcomes describe what students learn about and what they learn to, as a result of the teaching and learning in the course.'

Of course, they will tell us they are merely describing the curriculum; that they don't teach – or even *deliver key learnings* – in this language. But they do. In the course of the twentieth century, humanities education survived punishing encounters with both scientific objectivity and post-modern subjectivity, but it might not survive managerialism. Management language and management practices have drifted as far down as lower primary schools, where they show up in mission statements written by eight-year-olds in Grade Two, and in school reports that parents and students understand no better than the teachers alleged to have composed them. Schools – and even universities – might have seen it as their duty to offer some resistance to the general debasement of the language. Instead they acquiesced. They became *outcomes-based*.

'Oh that the Lord would show me how to think and how to choose!' It is difficult to find in the outcomes-based curriculum a better description of education's purpose or anything so well expressed. The question that no one seems able to answer is this: even if we had to change the way we organise educational institutions and adapt or discard older philosophies, did we have to give up teaching children to write and think in the language of that student writing in his diary 150 years ago?

* * *

Your child is exhibiting ALL key indicators.

School report

You are the parent of the child. Make a list of key indicators she has been exhibiting to you – then a list of the exhibits she's been indicating.

* * *

Essential Learnings identify what should be taught and what is important for students to have opportunities to know, understand and be able to do.

Queensland Education Department

Essential Learnings clearly focus attention on what
is central to the curriculum and help educators
determine what learners should know, understand,
value and be able to do.

Tasmanian Education Department

Can you think of a reason for the difference between
Queenslanders and Tasmanians? Or are their essential learnings
essentially the same?

Are your essential learnings different in this example?

The EsseNTial Learnings are organised into the Inner
Learner, Creative Learner, Collaborative Learner
and Constructive Learner domains. Each domain
has a set of culminating outcomes and developmental
indicators to help map a learner's progress through the
Key Growth Points and Bands.

Northern Territory Education Department

Do the capital N and T make any difference to the culminating
outcomes in your particular domain?

★ ★ ★

This paper presents the learnings from the CAT
Pilot and the POEM Pilot within the context of the
development of a youth transition system as envisaged
in the former Prime Minister Howards's Youth
Pathways Action Plan Taskforce report, Footprints to
the Future . . .

Among other things, the Taskforce found that:

- learning delivered in community settings, by a
  partnership involving education and community
  providers, offers the best possible opportunity for
  engaging disconnected young people in appropriate
  education.

Department of Education, Employment and Workplace Relations

How many words can you move around without changing the meaning of the last sentence? What IS the meaning of the last sentence?

* * *

LIFE: Learnings about suicide

www.health.gov.au

International evaluations of the High/Scope curriculum indicate that it produces high-quality results across a range of desired outcomes.

Early Childhood Australia

Outcomes: attainment of desired outcomes, not limited to results in tests are achievements of 'standards', but to include attitudinal measures, observations and anecdotes.

Warragul Regional College

Which of the following words best describes your feelings? i) relieved ii) puzzled iii) numb iv) tired v) any other word. Does the answer change if you read the sentences backwards?

* * *

Blueprint Sponsor Group

This group brings together key people across the Office of Education, the Office of Learning and Teaching and the Office of Strategy and Resources who are responsible for Blueprint strategies 3-7. The group meets regularly to ensure we develop a shared understanding of the core initiatives and to discuss key issues that emerge. By addressing the interdependencies of the initiatives, within the overarching framework of the Blueprint, the group is able to support a cohesive communication strategy to principals and schools. In addition, each construct requires the central office staff to engage deeply with the concepts that underpin each of the initiatives. A range of processes have been used to explore issues and gather feedback from different stakeholders to inform our thinking.

On a staff noticeboard

Summarise.

* * *

Class Mission Statement

Producing a mission statement is a process used for developing an agreed sense of purpose.

10. Have all students in the class sign the mission statement.

11. Laminate and display on door of classroom.

Program Achieve

Students' Habits of the Mind: time management, goal settings . . . reflective problem solving . . . internal locus of control for learning . . . risk taking

Code for Kids

Simplify and work with students using suggested tools e.g. brainstorming, consensogram, affinity program.

Complete activity by making a visual display of class rules.

Ormond Primary School, Grade 2

Make a visual display of your internal locus of control for learning and laminate it.

* * *

Learning Outcomes

At the end of the session, participants will be able to enhance their performance in negotiating and influencing situations, build on and further develop their current level of expertise, understand and be able to adapt an integral model and process for negotiating and influencing, understand how to read negotiating styles and develop personal behavioural flexibility, distinguish between process and content and understand where and how to leverage both.

OpenMind Research Group

Name one other possible outcome of the session.

* * *

We now effectively deliver the core business activities of the three previous bodies . . .

Being more responsive to the policy needs of government . . .

The QSF will help schools develop new and more flexible models for managing learning. This changing external environment, a quicker response to stakeholder needs and to reconsider the products and services offered by the QSA.

Email from Kim Bannikoff to all staff; subject: Development of the 2004–2006 strategic plan

i) Explain the relationship between the education of children and the last two sentences? ii) What is the core business activity of a school?

* * *

> In-service education is an ongoing thought-out school-based strategy co-operatively conceived and professionally executed to co-ordinate and exploit the in-built and developmental dimensions to comply with the well-known definition of the creativity of the school, geared towards self-renewal but not ignoring extra-mural influences.
>
> Resolved at a meeting with the Standing Committee for In-service Education, Queensland

Read this sentence, look away and answer this question in not more than twenty words: What is *in-service education*?

* * *

> Students will continue to consider the relationships between texts and to engage in the close reading of individual texts and wide reading of a range of different kinds of texts . . . The syllabus recognises the significance of meaning as a process as well as a result of responding to and composing texts.
>
> An Introduction to English Stage 6 in the New HSC, Board of Studies, NSW

Compose a text that explains what point about texts the author is making in his or her text.

* * *

Content

The new syllabus:

includes key competencies appropriate and relevant
to the study of English. They are developed through
the core processes of composing and responding
that underpin each course. The key competencies
are designed to enhance student learning within the
context of Stage 6 English makes explicit the learning
process and develops student ability to initiate,
monitor and reflect on various strategies of learning.

An Introduction to English Stage 6 in the New HSC, Board of Studies, NSW

Using your own favourite strategy of learning, explain what is
happening in this sentence.

* * *

The new syllabus requires a balance among:

- the assessment of knowledge and
  understanding outcomes, and skills outcomes
  syllabus components and language modes.

An Introduction to English Stage 6 in the New HSC, Board of Studies, NSW

In what language mode was this written?

* * *

He uses reading strategies that include selecting key ideas, paraphrasing and visualising the more complex sentences, reading on and drawing on some contextual cues . . . He is able to apply evidence from the text and his general knowledge to display literal, inferential and evaluative comprehension skills.

Louise Steb, Essendon, letter to *The Age*, 15 December 2008

Imagine you are a mother without a strategy for reading this school report. What would you say to your child?

* * *

1.3 Gap Analysis

It is inevitable in an organisation of around 1300 schools, there will be some differences between what individual schools are currently doing and the school's future practice. These differences form the *Gap Analysis* for each school.

1.4 School Readiness Assessment

For each difference identified in the *Gap Analysis* above, the degree of impact on the school itself will need to be considered. It is possible that some differences will have little impact on the school, while others will need to be explicitly managed to ensure a smooth transition.

1.5 School Change Management Plan

Details of each impact identified as having significant effect upon the school, will be summarised in the school's Change Management Plan. This will include a comparison of the current and future practice, as well as the impact upon the school and any activities that can or need to be undertaken to support the school and the school's staff. The impacts and activities are derived from the Gap Analysis and School Readiness Assessment. This plan will be generated automatically as a result of completing the questions in section 2.

Queensland Government – Department of Education, Training and the Arts.
OneSchool – Change Management – SCC Preparation, February 2008

Calculate the degree of impact on these sentences if other words were used in place of 'impact'. Explicitly manage to ensure a smooth transition.

* * *

NMIT Strategic Plan — the northern journey

CEO'S INTRODUCTION

I am pleased to introduce the new NMIT Strategic Plan, The Northern Journey . . . In this new Strategic Plan, NMIT has identified clear priorities and strategies to sustain our presence in the north and beyond and our obligations to our stakeholders, whilst also maintaining the capacity to respond flexibly to new opportunities as government, industry and community expectations change . . .

The NMIT Strategic Plan is organised around the themes of Learning, Engagement and Capacity, and these, with the identified key result areas, will provide the basis for planning and operations in the coming years . . .

Do you think this will work?

* * *

While the Smart Classrooms Coordinator (SCC) from each school will be responsible for the development of the Change Management Plan, they will not necessarily be responsible for undertaking the activities outlined in the plan. These are more likely to be undertaken by the same staff that helped detail the school's current practices . . .

Queensland Government, OneSchool Change Management

Why is the Smart Classrooms Coordinator not responsible for the activities?

★ ★ ★

Read the following extract carefully:

. . . The Indigenous Education Strategic Plan, developed by the Department of Employment, Education and Training, provides a road map for implementation of the vision I spoke about last year.

A strong and relevant education system that gets results for Indigenous Territorians is this government's number one priority. My vision is for a genuine partnership between Indigenous parents, students and those responsible for the education of young Indigenous Territorians with a view to better life outcomes for Indigenous people.

The gains in the educational outcomes of Indigenous students over the past five years have been heartening, and I commend all involved. This work can only now accelerate when genuine partnership between the education system and Indigenous Territorians exists.

I commend this strategic plan and the future it represents.

Syd Stirling, Minister for Employment, Education and Training, *Indigenous Education Strategic Plan 2006–2009 – NT*

Write a letter to the minister asking what 'gains in the educational outcomes of Indigenous students over the past five years' have heartened him?

* * *

Achieving quantum improvements in educational outcomes needs alignment of effort from everyone in the department, in coordination with our stakeholders. Most importantly, our efforts must be based on a genuine respect for Indigenous Territorians.

I am committed to this strategic plan and look forward to working with you on its successful implementation.

Chief Executive, Department of Employment, Education and Training. *Indigenous Education Strategic Plan 2006–2009 – NT*

You are a parent in the Northern Territory: on a scale of one to ten, as a description of your child's needs where would you rank 'alignment of effort from everyone in the department, in coordination with our stakeholders'?

* * *

Read the following Northern Territory Education Department Executive Summary:

2. *Executive Summary*

VISION

DEET's vision is for Indigenous people to fully influence and participate in the social and economic future of the Northern Territory and the wider Australian community.

DEET's contribution to this vision is outlined in

the following three major sections of this plan:

1) Outcomes: The Outcomes section discusses the results that DEET wants from this strategy. It includes a discussion about the major issues in each of the five outcome areas.

2) Action Areas and Priorities: The Action Areas section discusses each of the six broad areas of DEET activity. It discusses the priorities that DEET will focus on delivering over the next four years.

3) Impact Framework: The Impact Framework section discusses how DEET will implement the strategy. This includes how DEET will monitor the progress of the activity, the impact of that activity on the desired outcomes and continuous evaluation to determine whether effort is directed in the areas that will have the greatest impact.

Indigenous Education Strategic Plan 2006–2009 – NT

Can you see the word teacher? Anywhere?

* * *

Focus rigorously on these words for two minutes:

DEET will progress Indigenous education by rigorously focussing on implementing priority actions . . .

Priorities:

1. Literacy and Numeracy Programs

Increase the focus on the development and methods for delivery of sustainable high quality school literacy and numeracy programs . . .

8. Health Stakeholder Agreements

Develop and implement agreements with stakeholders

to establish and maintain working relationships
between schools and health providers

Indigenous Education Strategic Plan 2006–2009 – NT

Stop focusing rigorously. Has anything happened? Maintain
your focus and sense of urgency in implementing an evaluation
of the following 'impact framework':

3. Impact Framework

The Impact Framework outlines how DEET
will maintain its focus and sense of urgency in
implementing this plan.

Action Areas	Priorities
A. RESOURCING AND IMPLEMENTING ACTIONS	1. Implement Strategic Plan Develop and implement effective school and corporate action plans. 2. Allocation of Resources Allocate new resources and redistribute existing resources on the basis of rigorous evaluation and analysis.
B. CRITICAL ANALYSIS AND REPORTING	3. Measure, Analyse and Drive Progress Critically analyse and progress reports, champion the strategy and challenge operational obstacles.
C. RESEARCH AND EVALUATION	4. Research and Evaluation Framework Introduce a research and evaluation framework to address knowledge gaps and provide an evidence base to determine what does, and does not, work.

Indigenous Education Strategic Plan 2006–2009 – NT

Focus on the wheel below with a sense of urgency. Can you feel it yet?

THE INDIGENOUS EDUCATION STRATEGIC PLAN 2006-2009
'The Action Wheel'

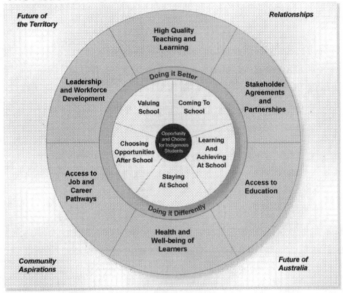

The Indigenous Education Strategic Plan **Action Wheel** incorporates:

☐ Outcomes – the inner circle.　　☐ Action Areas – the outer circle.

The **Action Wheel** illustrates the interrelationship between the outcomes and the action areas: achievement in any one action area will impact on more than one desired outcome, conversely, achieving sustainable outcomes requires activity in more than one action area.

The **Action Wheel** also guides implementation of the strategy beyond the systemic priorities identified in the plan. The **Action Wheel** permits a school, or corporate division, to prioritise the actions and outcomes according to the needs of its clients or the specifics of its context. Depending on what the issue is (which outcome is most important), it is possible to align the outcome against any of the six Action Areas to develop specialised and localised activities that will address that outcome. This is discussed further in *Section 5: Impact Framework*.

The four cornerstones supporting the **Action Wheel** remind us that improving opportunity and choice for Indigenous students is important for the future of the Territory and Australia, and that achieving the vision will require strong relationships that support the aspirations of the Indigenous community.

Read the first two paragraphs beneath the Action Wheel. See how many more outcomes you can add without changing the meaning. For example: 'The Action Outcome Wheel also guides implementation of the outcome beyond the systemic priorities and outcomes identified in the plan (outcome).'

Read the third paragraph. In you own words, how does the Action Wheel remind us of that which they say it does?

* * *

MGTS delivers training that is responsive to the needs of employers and industry in the 21st century. It is never content to 'rest on its laurels' and its focus is on continuous improvement in every aspect of its work.

Midland Group Training Service

Why are there inverted commas around 'rest on its laurels'?

* * *

As the Monitoring & Evaluation Adviser the key focus will be to support the ongoing implementation of ECBP monitoring and evaluation frameworks to meet reporting requirements . . . applicants will need to demonstrate significant experience in best practice monitoring and evaluation . . . An understanding of mainstreaming gender and HIV/AIDS in this context will be well regarded.

Education Capacity Building Program, Port Moresby.

Give three reasons why PNG will be a better place if the key focus is maintained.

* * *

The Premier, John Brumby, today declared Victoria at the forefront of the education revolution, launching a bold, five-year education reform agenda designed to deliver excellence in schools . . .

'Our Government is committed to lifting up all schools to a standard of excellence . . . These reforms show that Victoria is leading the way nationally when it comes to education and that we are education revolution-ready . . . we are now ready and willing as the first State to drive the implementation of that reform . . . We have also announced a $10 million Institute of Educational Leadership will be established to develop current and aspiring school leaders, because great leadership drives excellence in the classroom.'

Premier of Victoria's website

1. Imagine you are not excited by the foregoing, and explain why.
2. Imagine you are excited and explain why.

★ ★ ★

This program is designed for specialist TAFE staff wanting to gain a greater understanding of the theories and practices relevant to personal and managerial competencies including individual learning styles, self management, integrating managerial competencies with development and facilitating a learning environment. Staff will gain a greater self awareness and receive useful tools to increase their effectiveness in both the workplace and their personal life.

TDC – Specialist Series: Improving your personal effectiveness

1. Describe your individual learning style.
2. Name three useful tools that staff will receive.

★ ★ ★

The role of the SCC is not necessarily to understand the details of the workings of the school. The role does, however, require an ability to be able to find the relevant information from other staff members who do understand how the school operates . . .

Queensland Government, OneSchool Change Management

What sort of course should the SCC attend? What is an SCC? Guess.

★ ★ ★

I'm asking you today to consider partnering once more with your University to achieve ongoing transformations.

In a letter from the University of Melbourne's 'Advancement Office'

Changing only one word, use this sentence in a letter to your mother or boyfriend.

★ ★ ★

In 2007 the University will continue the successful scheme of Quality Initiatives Grants. These grants assist groups to research/develop and/or implement a quality improvement initiative. Projects may be initiated from any organisational unit within the University . . .

Quality Initiative Grants support the development, pilot or introductory phase of an activity and proposals are assessed in terms of the following criteria:

- the feasibility of what is proposed, including the appropriateness of the plan, timescale and resources applied to the project

- demonstration of a clear link between the funding

proposals and the Quality Improvement Plans of the Organisational unit as a whole . . .

La Trobe University

Using the University's description as a guide, describe:
1. A Quality Initiative Grant
2. A Quality Improvement Plan
3. A Quality Improvement Initiative

* * *

Janine's learnings from this experience, which were:

- To seek conceptual frameworks — literature and explicated concepts can help to get a 'helicopter' perspective. This, she gained through her readings, reflections and discussions with her researcher/ sounding board.

Janine's strategy to model relationship-based leadership and reflective practice was a profound statement of her leadership intentions for the District. If this strategy is successful — even marginally — it will bring a positive change in organisation culture in the District.

Janine was at a Women in Leadership course with the Western Australian Department of Education

What was Janine's 'profound statement'?

* * *

We are driving towards developing key statements leading towards the improved visualisation of our school . . . We want the image we create to be representative of our key statements. It is part of getting our symbolisation into the community.

Acting principal of a public school in Dee Why, Sydney

In what ways might a 'helicopter' perspective help the Acting
Principal?

* * *

> *The Knowledge Tree: an e-Journal of Learning Innovation* is a
> leading journal of e-learning. It was originally an
> e-journal in flexible learning produced through
> the Flexible Learning Leaders Project of the
> Framework . . . As the organisation producing
> and publishing the content of *The Knowledge Tree*, you
> will be required to: Provide strategic thinking for
> continuous improvement . . . Research widely in
> the area of innovative and embedding practices of
> e-learning in the VET system and across educational
> sectors . . . Network, liaise and collaborate with
> stakeholders . . . Use *The Knowledge Tree* to 'capture' and
> extend knowledge shared in online networks, CoPs
> and forums and f2f activities focused on e-learning.

EOI (expression of interest) from the Australian Flexible Learning Framework

Capture three innovative and embedding practices of e-learning.

* * *

Schools enacting Rich Tasks and the QCAR Framework Schools enacting Rich Tasks are well placed to implement the QCAR Framework. The 5 main deliverables of QCAR have, in a sense, already arrived in Rich Task schools:

- Essential Learnings

- Assessment bank

- Standards–based assessment

- Common assessment tasks

- Reports.

The Rich Task to Essential Learnings Mapper (Version 2) A computer–based tool for mapping the alignment of Rich Tasks and the draft Essential Learnings. The mapper was developed as a pragmatic response to the need for teachers to demonstrate how their enactments of the Rich Tasks, Blueprint tasks or school–developed tasks satisfy systemic requirements under the QCAR framework.

Queensland Department of Education, Training and the Arts

Using your computer–based tool, create a pragmatic mapper.

* * *

The barriers to achieving effective knowledge transfer

Literature on knowledge sharing identified numerous barriers that impede the effective exchange of knowledge (O'Dell & Grayson, 1998; Hazel Hall, 2002a; Martin, 2003; Truch, 2001, Lancaster, 2003; Huysman, 2003; Hendriks, 2004).

Examples of barriers are:

- individuals' dispositional impediments, often translating into action or lack of action, such as people not knowing what they know, what knowledge might be helpful for others, or what knowledge exists; people considering that knowledge does not apply to them; people withholding information, 'bad news' knowledge or intellectual property

- management practices, such as locking up tacit knowledge, denying time to engage in transfer, or failing to implement knowledge once it is transferred, limiting relationships or extending 'distances' between knowledge exchange partners

Clayton and Fisher

What knowledge have Clayton and Fisher shared with us? Name three colleagues and their dispositional impediments, and one who denies time to engage in transfer.

* * *

Functional and Traditional Grammar

The QSA Grammar Scope and Sequence that accompanies the English Essentials and Standards is underpinned by a functional model of language, but foregrounds traditional grammar terminology.

QCARupdate newsletter, March 2008, Queensland Department of Education, Training and the Arts

Would you say the language of this sentence is underpinned by a functional model, or does it foreground traditional grammar terminology? Or both?

* * *

This edition of Research eLert explores the concept of 'value-added' measures as a means of measuring how schools are progressing in improving student learning outcomes . . . These international models demonstrate how value-added measures can be used as a tool for school improvement . . .

Education Policy and Research Division, Office for Education Policy and Innovation, Victoria

Would value be added or lost if one these sentences were deleted?

★ ★ ★

Student priorities are issues arising from the contributing feedback processes and are generally underlying causal issues being different from specific issues identified and addressed within the contributing feedback process.

University Student Priorities Policy and Process, Edith Cowan University

Without looking – what are student priorities?

★ ★ ★

Describe your school's procedures for teachers to manage and record behaviour incidents in the classroom. What are the school's procedures for teachers to manage and record behaviour incidents outside the classroom? e.g. playground, excursion etc.

Queensland Government, OneSchool Change Management

In no more than 500 words, describe a behaviour incident you have observed or in which you have participated – 600 if bones were broken or lives lost.

★ ★ ★

Discussion was held on the draft Middleware and Action Plan Strategy Roadmap that had been recently released for comment. Outcomes from the discussion were:

   . . . Emphasis appears to be lacking on the value-add of Teaching and Learning collaboration as by-product . . .

West Australian Regional Network Organisation

Does this strike you as an important outcome? Why?

* * *

The Institute Board held a successful workshop with the Executive Team last week. The main item discussed was the long term planning on the Institute's physical footprint.

. . .

This training has been designed to facilitate the smooth implementation of the six strategic change projects the Institute is currently developing. These change projects are strategically important in moving the organisation forward and it is vital that they are implemented in an effective and non threatening way. To remind you these projects will be defined under the following headings;

- Silos

- Communication

- Role Clarity

- Optimal Systems and Processes

- Business Case Methodology

- Demand Driven Education and Training

From two emails to staff from an acting CEO

Construct your own strategic Action Plan Roadmap and implement it in a threatening way.

★ ★ ★

> Policies for knowledge transfer: There was general acknowledgement that sharing of critical knowledge is an issue, even when the first step — identifying critical knowledge — has not been taken.
>
> **Clayton and Fisher**

Estimate how much Clayton and Fisher were paid for their work.

★ ★ ★

> The Knowledge Management (KM) Steering Committee which was formed to provide support for the direction of Knowledge Management in the Institute, has sponsored several small projects designed to progress the Knowledge Management strategy of the Institute . . . As the climate of educational delivery changes, we need to be more responsive to opportunities and develop our capacity to change and be at the forefront of training and education in our region. Knowledge Management is a key strategy in achieving this result.
>
> **Grant Sutherland, CEO of the Gordon Institute of TAFE**

What does the author mean by 'the climate of educational delivery'?

★ ★ ★

Is it possible to evaluate dynamic, complex, unpredictable, multifaceted, emergent processes where there is a shift from highly structured and linear professional learning and development to embedding enablers that support confident, capable, connected, curious and committed learners?

NSW Department of Education and Training

Write your answer here:

* * *

Narre Warren South P-12 College aims to create an Ongoing Learning Community which cares, stimulates and ensures opportunities for equality and growth by responding to individual needs, whilst sharing collective responsibility for building and sustaining an optimum Learning and Teaching environment.

What is the difference between an Ongoing Learning Community and an Ongoing school?

* * *

Over 2000 users from 'early adopter' areas have already been migrated, with many expressing high levels of satisfaction with their newly gained functionality.

Melbourne University Staff News, March 2007

Are you at present satisfied with your functionality?

* * *

There are many Domain area specific
initiatives . . . All policies have an operational
aspect . . . Domain Leaders were asked to develop and
implement strategies to lift student performance at
all levels (one target being) The Managed Individual
Pathways Program.

From the Principal's Report, published in the Dandenong High School Awards Night
program, December 2006

Should Dandenong High School become an Ongoing
Learning Community?

★ ★ ★

This is part of the development of an audience-
centred information architecture . . . The information
architecture itself was the result of extensive
consultation with stakeholders . . .

Deputy Vice Chancellor (Academic), University of New England, on its new
homepage

Imagine you are a stakeholder in an audience-centred
information architecture – prepare a series of PowerPoint slides
that illustrate your stakeholder interest.

★ ★ ★

Review and assessment of existing capacity has
been under review and consideration by executive
management of Curtin over the course of the year as
it became increasingly evident that Curtin needed to
address critical strategic imperatives and positioning
within the changed, dynamic higher education
environment and government climate.

Professor Gregory Craven, A/Deputy Vice-Chancellor, Curtin University of
Technology

Review and consider the review and assessment of climate described. Name four non-critical imperatives.

* * *

Students read, view, discuss, analyse and respond critically to imaginative, informative and persuasive texts in a range of media text types. These include contemporary, classical and popular texts, documentaries, reviews and texts in the workplace. They use literal, inferential and evaluative comprehension to identify multiple perspectives. They explain the ways that texts could change if set in different sociocultural contexts. They identify the differences between media text types and infer by whom and for whom texts were written. They identify the significance of symbols that have specific cultural or chronological meaning within texts. They compare and contrast the typical features or conventions of different media text types, including the use of imagery, stereotyping and symbolism.

One of twelve paragraphs in an email to clarify what should be taught in Year 7 English, taken from Victoria's new VELS (Victorian Essential Learning Standards)

While preserving the meaning of this text, rewrite it using the word 'text' no more than twice. What *is* the meaning of this text?

* * *

. . . strategies aimed at alleviating dysfunctional conflict outcomes.

Western Australian Education Department

Describe a dysfunctional conflict outcome that you have witnessed. Was it alleviated?

★ ★ ★

> The AHRC has announced the decision to end its support for resource enhancement through the discrete responsive-mode scheme, but to continue to support the enhancement of research resources alongside a process of research within the Research Grants scheme, and to establish a scheme in strategic mode through a series of communication activities with the community.
>
> The Arts and Humanities Research Council (AHRC) Strategic Resource Enhancement Programme in the United Kingdom

Does this strike you as a good idea?

★ ★ ★

> Investigate how language has been used to construct representations of the artefacts and iconography of a particular culture in a range of texts, considering to what extent the texts are constructed in socially valued modes, and the ways they employ representations to reflect, reinforce or challenge dominant ideologies in terms of what social groups are included or excluded from a sense of community. Present your findings in a PowerPoint, with accompanying written text.
>
> Sample Investigation Task for English from the WA Curriculum Council

Go on – do it.

★ ★ ★

Our staff and students will be: entrepreneurial in their endeavours – generating innovative ideas . . . which will deliver a Swinburne by 2015 . . . that is engaged with industry and community underpinned by a commitment to a sustainable Swinburne.

Swinburne University of Technology, Statement of Direction 2015

What do you think the author means by 'underpinned by a commitment to a sustainable Swinburne'?

* * *

. . . the challenges and worries will turn to excitement . . . Design and Technology will be reborn – evolve as a forward thinking vibrant learning subject.

President of the Design & Technology Teachers' Association's magazine

What do you think the author means by:

i) reborn

ii) forward thinking learning subject

iii) challenges

* * *

The purpose is to equip us better to achieve the 'ambition inspired by achievement' which underpins our new strategic plan . . . It is now imperative that we define the pathways, the priorities and the performance indicators that will make a reality . . . This position is intended to optimise the feedback loop in which energy and initiative at the 'cutting edge' is encouraged and also shapes and is influenced by corporate strategies.

The University of Sydney's new organisational structure

Using a diagram show:

- how ambition is inspired by achievement and not the other way round and:

- how energy and initiative in the feedback loop does all those things.

* * *

A further important element of the Growing Esteem strategy is knowledge transfer – the third strand of Growing Esteem's 'triple helix' . . . This year we will work to embed knowledge transfer into the core work of the University . . .

Melbourne Update, The University of Melbourne

Can you think of another way to say this? Or is it too late?

* * *

In 2005 Yarrawonga Secondary College (YSC) underwent substantial changes to the leadership structure with the appointment of a new Principal Class team. During this time it became evident that the College needed a clear direction, vision and common focus . . . Responses were collated and we engaged the services of an outside facilitator to run a whole day and whole school (teaching & SSO staff) Professional learning day focusing on setting our vision, values, mission for staff and aims for students, using the responses already gained from staff. (See Appendix 3: Visioning Workshop with whole staff) . . . The school applied for a values grant to assist in embedding our values at the College . . . The College adopted Restorative Practice as the means by which student support and management is to be handled. Staff are to be held accountable to our aims, mission and values. We will strive to do fewer things better and to align all teaching, learning and activity to our school aims, values and mission.

> Values Education for Australian Schooling: The values journey at Yarrawonga Secondary College

You were a student at the visioning workshop. Write an essay that explains why it was the best day of your life.

* * *

At the Queensland University of Technology – the 'Master of Education' course has become the 'Master of Learning Innovation'.

> www.weaselwords.com.au

Why?

* * *

James Cook University commits itself to: establishing consistency between stated objectives and the content, teaching interactions and assessment tasks of all subjects. As part of this commitment, students will receive adequate and prompt feedback on their assessed work so that with support from teaching staff they can adjust their learning practices to achieve the stated objectives.

> 'Principles of Good Assessment – Guidelines for Teaching Staff', James Cook University

Adjust your own learning practice.

★ ★ ★

Are your learning practices in order to appropriately respond to the following strategic pillars?

Our Strategic Pillars

In attempting to formulate solutions to address our strategic issues, we needed to create a focus for our activities whilst maintaining core activities. This was accomplished through the creation of Pillars. Pillars, in the CQU context, are those areas where we need to concentrate in order to adequately and appropriately respond to our identified strategic issues.

Central Queensland University Strategic Plan

★ ★ ★

The co-curricular activities are designed to allow the girls to take their place as global citizens . . . the building program places its learning environment at the forefront of educational design.

Ruyton Girls' School

If this were all you knew about Ruyton Girls' School, would you send your daughter there?

★ ★ ★

As we enter into 2006 I am confident that a number of developments of a strategic sort will begin to drive the School's agenda in the short to medium term . . .

On the research front, five emerging teams of researchers suggest that the School has intrinsic nodes of research strength worth developing further . . . The School finds itself thrust into a 'force-field' that gives great weight to research teams more than ever . . .

Also, disciplines will want to reassess whether conducting tutorials for advanced courses is really 'best practice' . . .

Lines of communication in the School need serious attention, especially as we tool up for the coming of the government's RQF regime in 2007. All members of the School will be encouraged to use the electronic UQ Calendar to foster increased communication . . .

'Morale boosting' open letter from the Head of the School of History, Philosophy, Religion and Classics at the University of Queensland, following a 'change management' restructure that resulted in the 'voluntary separation' of five and a half members of staff

Read the Head of School's letter carefully. Write a satire of your own.

* * *

The methodology promotes effective management and governance of projects by constantly reviewing the business case with stakeholders at key decision points in the project lifecycle. It provides a transparent framework for communication about project progress, processes, issues, and risks . . . a strong focus on business benefits and provides a standard method to clearly define project outcomes or products . . .

Macquarie University

What does the methodology promote?

* * *

Following a recent restructure in a community-based NGO, the Library has become a Learning Centre and the librarian is a Knowledge Coordinator.

How soon should we expect to see the benefits of this initiative?

* * *

Unit standard: a nationally registered, coherent set of learning outcomes and associated performance criteria, together with technical and management information that supports delivery and assessment.

From the New Zealand Qualifications Authority

What word best describes your state of mind after reading this?

* * *

All lecturer and tutors at Australian International University are SSP's. SSP stands for 'Subcontracted Service Provider'. The utilisation of SSP teachers keeps costs as low as possible for us. We can then pass on these cost savings to you, our valued clients.

The Australian International University

Imagine you are an SSP. Do you feel utilised by this?

* * *

Any communication strategy needs to be multi-layered and very flexible and dynamic.

From the Report of the Ministerial Task Force on Issues Surrounding Proposed Changes to Post-Compulsory Education, July 2005

Do you agree or disagree?

* * *

It will take a specific angle on the effects of institutional policies on individuals and be based on a range of texts that communicate various attitudes and beliefs about such effects.

It will explore the questions of what these attitudes and beliefs are and how the texts communicate ideas about institutions and their beliefs on individuals.

From an HSC English assessment task titled 'Write a Feature Article', New South Wales

Explain why this task makes you want to be a journalist?

* * *

An information factory, supported by a data warehouse would provide the longitudinal information needed for improving education in Arizona.

Arizona Educational Technology Plan Adding the Sixth 'C' to the Economic Picture 2002–2007

Is it the same where you live?

* * *

From an end-user perspective, initially, there should be little change in the service. Moving forward Facilities and Services will be developing a more user focussed and performance-driven cleaning regime across the campus.

Monash University's 'New Cleaning Structure'

Describe, in your own words, a user-focused cleaning regime.

* * *

Colleagues: As you are aware NSI is reviewing its Business Lines to improve the performance and sustainability of the Institute by strengthening the value adding connection between and across the customer service points. During the course of this project, roles and responsibilities of Business Lines will be clarified and the dimensions of Business Lines will be revisited. An operating model will be developed to enable NSI to achieve planned outcomes through the development of products and services, marketing and selling of products and services, and the customer relations and delivery of products and services. Efforts will be clustered to match the defined customer profile groups and to capitalise on the changing market environment and emerging opportunities.

Northern Sydney Institute of TAFE Director

Give an example. Remember to cluster your efforts.

★ ★ ★

The Productive Pedagogies project is the first stage of the learning and development program to support curriculum renewal, through the curriculum framework planning process, in all Queensland schools and is a strategy to engage schools in professional development in Productive Pedagogies and productive assessment.

Education Queensland

Does this sentence strike you as a product of Productive Pedagogies? What about this one?

Candidates: make decisions about the appropriateness and effectiveness of the staging of texts and the sequencing and organisation of subject matter, and of the use of cohesive ties to link ideas in a range of texts, including those that are multigeneric and multimodal; use a range of sentence and clause structures, and use grammar, as appropriate to purposes, cultural context, and social situations; deploy paragraphing and punctuation and control spelling as appropriate to and effective for particular purposes in particular cultural contexts and social situations.

External Senior English Syllabus, Queensland Studies Authority

* * *

Since the focus of the Australian Flexible Learning Framework for this year is embedding e-learning and engaging clients, here's an exciting opportunity to re-energise the change process by focusing on what is working well and then amplifying it . . . Appreciative Inquiry is a strength-based process which engages a range of stakeholders in collaboratively identifying what is working well then compiling those compelling features into a system for positive change.

From a Staff Training & Development Officer at TAFENSW Riverina Institute

Conduct an Appreciative Inquiry into these sentences, then compile the compelling features.

* * *

The twenty-first century challenge is to find a cross-cultural methodology to speed up ideation for this purpose without sacrificing the creativity and humanity of our ideas. Creative Aerobics (CA) is an evolutionary multi-cultural, time-sensitive, process-driven heuristic paradigm I designed that utilizes new methodologies to generate new messages in a fraction of the time required by traditional creative approaches. CA employs semiotics, the literary and less-than-literary, and the art of engagement. By completing four mental exercises in succession that increase the flexibility of information exchange between left and right brain, CA users develop multiple approaches, strategies, markets and solutions they can utilize for the assignment at hand — fresher, more persuasive outside-the-box solutions.

Linda Conway Correll, Assistant Professor, College of Journalism, Department of Advertising, University of Florida. From the workshop titled 'New Directions in Global Commercial Communication: Creative Aerobics: The Art of Ideation'

Do you doubt any of Professor Conway's claims? What do you think she is talking about?

★ ★ ★

The culmination of a dynamic mixture of developmental and discipline based content that is connected to performance indicators and congruent opportunity to learn standards.

Education Queensland

Culminated in what, do you think?

* * *

Meta–frame this:

> Giving a macro, big–picture interpretation by
> helicoptering above an issue.
>
> Explanation of 'meta-frame' from former Director General, Education Queensland

* * *

> 3.1 Facilitative communication skills are utilised
> to asist the client to identify areas of concern, to
> prioritise areas for immediate and longer term action
> and to determine options for action and workable
> strategies to address their priority areas.
>
> Performance criterion – unit of competency
> CHCCS402A: Respond holistically to client issues.
>
> Community Services Training Packages, www.ntis.gov.au

Respond holistically, using facilitative communication skills.

* * *

Develop an appropriate operating model to enable you to
ask your own questions of the next examples. Cluster your
efforts to answer them in a caring learning environment with
appropriate scaffolding.

> Generalist university administrator and a specialist
> information disseminator.
>
> The skills of a public relations officer employed at a university

> Riverina Institute has made a commitment to the
> Department of Commerce to provide statistical data
> of current usage patterns and the type of products
> purchased in relation to the washroom consumables.
>
> Email from a NSW Department of Education Regional Administration Manager;
> subject: Washroom Consumables Usage

The aim of the Department of Education and Children's Services (DECS) is to achieve quality learning and wellbeing outcomes for children and students in its children's services, preschools and government schools. In order to do this, DECS is developing connecting roles and interdependencies throughout the organisation.

From a booklet called 'Putting the Jigsaw Together:
DECS Roles and Interdependencies', produced by the SA Dept of Education and Children's Services

The network has progressed towards achieving its aim with stakeholders to develop strategic partnerships to keep young people engaged in education, training or employment.

Outer Eastern Local Learning Employment Network, 2003 Annual Report

When introduced, market-based competition was expected to result in improved choice and diversity, efficiency, responsiveness, quality, flexibility, innovation, and access and equity within vocational education and training.

The National Centre for Vocational Education Research

This approach to the contexts requires accurate whole of program mapping and planning and the core learning outcomes as the endorsed core curriculum should be used as reference points to ensure a realignment of contexts is appropriate for particular core learning outcomes and for particular bands of schooling.

Studies of Society and Environment (SOSE): Planning considerations for the Years I to 10 Syllabus, Queensland Studies Authority

I understand that the focus on customer relations and a desire to provide quality services results from the ethos and culture of the company . . . and throughout all areas of operation.

Principal, Adelaide High School

Where the responses are from a list, the Change Management Plan will offer some reasonably specific support for managing the change at the school . . .

Queensland Government, OneSchool Change Management

★ ★ ★

Within Greg's new role he will be responsible for the AQTF implementation across BRIT along with the management of the Teaching Excellence Project, Teaching Fellowship initiative and educational capability building including implantation of some TAFE Development Centre projects.

Email to TAFE staff

What will Greg do in his new role? And Doug – will he be very busy?

During this period, Doug will undertake duties that will enable the Institute to better manage and track our training activity against all fund sources and reporting codes as well as take advantage of any new government funded initiatives. This will include a review of the type of reports that we currently give operational managers within the teaching centers to track their progress against target, with a greater emphasis on responding to a demand driven system in both government funded and fee for service areas, including international programs. The importance of this type of work cannot be underestimated as our sector moves into a new even more competitive environment.

Email to TAFE staff

* * *

Doug will be located in A1.11b when Gerald returns
to his TLQ role in January, his contact details will
remain the same. I know everyone will welcome Doug
as he undertakes to work with them in his new role,
I am very happy that he has agreed to be the 'guinea
pig ' and look forward to working closely with him
to ensure the Institute progresses the opportunities
that user choice will bring us. You will already have
received an email from Brad, which among other
items, outlines the backfill arrangements for Doug's
substantive position in 2009.

Email to TAFE staff

What sort of backfill arrangements would you make?

* * *

Performance development and data protocols

A survey of Learning Circles suggests that all but
three or four teachers have, or are within a day or
two, of signing off their plans with Leading Teachers.
Thanks to everyone for their participation in the
process, which makes a significant contribution to the
clarification of our collective goals and professional
learning needs. Attached you will find an updated
Professional Learning Policy, based on one developed
in 2002. Most updates reflect the philosophy of the
Performance Development Culture and current
thinking on effective professional learning.

Warragul Regional College

Imagine you are one of the three or four teachers: in no more
than 500 words, explain why you haven't signed off.

* * *

Our school facilitates and implements a comprehensive curriculum, developed from eight key learning areas, that engages students in developing the essentials of lifelong learning within a safe, tolerant and disciplined environment. Through clear, delineated learning outcomes aligned to the developmental level of students, they are empowered to communicate, create, reflect, investigate, understand and participate effectively in our multiliterate, global society.'

Gordonvale State School's statement of purpose

Is Gordonvale school doing enough? What else might it try?

* * *

Mediated punishment

If proactive focus on counselling and mediation fails to stop the ill-treatment of one person towards another a range of sanctions will be used to assist the elimination of the behaviour.

The principal takes calculated risks based on cost benefit analysis to obtain resources to enhance school effectiveness.

Warragul Regional College

Health

Management has invaded the health business. Why should those awaiting a *birth event* or fearing a *death event* or some other *adverse patient outcome* expect to be spared? If a waiter can ask a healthy customer if his banana split is *inactive*, why can't a nurse ask a demented old soul if he *ambulates*? Is he not entitled to be treated as a customer like everybody else? Why should the old and deranged be treated like second-class customers? Their money is as good as anybody's. Why can't doctors live the brand too? Why shouldn't residents of nursing homes and drug-rehabilitation facilities and burns units be as loyal as any other clients?

★ ★ ★

Recreate this meeting in Belfast as a play, a burlesque or an episode of *Grey's Anatomy*:

> NORTHERN IRELAND PRACTICE AND EDUCATION COUNCIL FOR NURSING AND MIDWIFERY (NIPEC)

> DEVELOPMENT FRAMEWORK FOR NURSES AND MIDWIVES

Minutes of Project Group

14 May 2004 at 9.30 am

Present: . . .

1: Apologies . . .

2: Minutes of the Previous Meeting dated 7 April 2004 . . .

6: Evaluation Scheme of the Development Framework Project

6.1: Brendan McGrath identified the proposed process for the evaluation. The Project Evaluation has been structured using the following framework:

- Project Management structures and progress reporting

- Delivery of significant milestones identified in the project plan

- Quality assurance of project outputs

- Evidence of rigor

- Partnership development

- Risk management

6.2: Paddie then elaborated regarding the above and identified that Edmund Thom (Head of Corporate Services for NIPEC), will be leading this Evaluation Scheme . . .

7: Feedback from Sub-Groups

7.1: Learning and Portfolio Sub-Group

Lesley reported that the group had identified a range of learning activities and related categories and that they would develop a brief descriptor of each activity, limited to available supporting literature, to aid the understanding of the range of learning activities identified. They will provide guidance for employers and individuals on how to make the most of these learning activities in relation to improving performance and role development. The categories of learning activities they identified are as follows:

- Learning from organizational perspectives

- Learning from adverse events

- Formal/traditional learning

- Learning from others

- Learning with others

- Experiential learning
  See attached Learning & Portfolio Sub-Group report.
  7.2: Performance and Competency Sub-Group

Tanya stated that within the Sub-Group they developed the Poor Performance definition and have linked it with the Performance definition which includes capability, willingness and opportunity to perform. Tanya asked Cathy to distribute the draft paper prepared by the Sub-Group regarding Definitions to be sent to all Project Group members asking them for their comments and feedback.

Tanya then gave 5 underpinning values which the Sub-Group identified.

- Accountability

- Leadership

- Continuous improvement

- Person centeredness

- Integrity
  These are necessary in using the competency Framework. There will be 5 – 6 Core Competencies against the 7 competency areas. See attached Sub-Group report for further detail.

It was also agreed that Paddie Blaney will chair the Performance and Competency Sub-Group when Tanya McCance is on Maternity leave.

See attached Sub-Group report.

7.3: Roles and Careers Sub-Group:

Working on the theme of 'Broad Role Development' the Sub-group reported that there was a lack of literature relating to this particular subject and thus they had explored some strategic documents particularly 'Developing Better Services'. Refer to attached Sub-Group report.

The Project Group felt that the Sub-Group had focused too much on the Competencies required for Broader Role Development rather than the Principles to guide a manager when considering developments of this type.

Following discussion Kay Kane suggested a four stage framework.

1. Why is the role Development required
2. In what way will this be developed
3. What factors need to be in place
4. How will/should this change be managed

Paddie suggested that the Sub-Groups also consider definitions for Individual And Broader Role Development.

Pat McGreevy referenced literature detailing a 'Strategic Staircase' This may be useful for Sub-Group to review. Tanya commented that she was able to see the link with the Competency Framework.

Brendan may use the Project Team to do some more detailed work.

8: Any other business

8.1: It was agreed by the remaining members of the Project Group that at the next Project Group meeting of 16 June 2004 each chair of the Sub-Groups will do

a 20 minute presentation for the whole of the Project
Group regarding updates of ongoing work within the
Sub-Groups.

This will help inform all of the Project Group
members of on going work. It was decided that this
will take place on 16 June 2004 from 9.30 am –
10.30 am . . .

8.2: Cathy informed the members that this will be
Tanya's last Project Group meeting before going on
maternity leave. Paddie commended the input and
contribution Tanya had made to date and this was also
commended by all the members of the Sub-Group.
Everyone wished her well . . .

* * *

Audit spiral

Surgeons will be familiar with the audit cycle, although
the aim is an audit spiral as a cycle will return the
participant to the starting point rather than to a higher
level.

The opening sentence of a 2006 surgical mortality report

Measurable solutions over an extended timeframe

Churchill Consulting and its staff have assisted a number of healthcare organisations to improve their market knowledge and implement measurable solutions to achieve their organisational objectives . . .

Churchill Consulting has assisted a major healthcare insurer to define and implement a channel strategy to improve their knowledge of the market as well as securing a long-term vision for how they will interact with customers as technology and customer preferences change . . .

. . . understand their market share.

. . . improve their share of the market . . .

. . . team more aligned and valuable to the business.

. . . review. . . implement. . . improve . . . ensure . . . validate . . . manage . . .

. . . robust programme office and project management capability.

This involved liaison with Government and funding bodies as well as modelling the supply and demand for medical practitioners on the Island of Ireland over an extended time-frame.

Churchill Consultants

Blue ocean

Product leadership or lowest-cost value propositions remain valid sources of competitive advantage, however for many businesses it is customer intimacy that affords them 'blue ocean' in their competitive waters.

Churchill Consultants

Cascading

Cascading works like this: when the benefit limit for one family member has been reached and a further benefit is then denied, some medical practitioners will submit a claim in another family member's name instead. Cascading therefore results in the payment of a benefit that is often not legitimate.

Senator Cory Bernardi, *Hansard*, 18 October 2006

Cleaner

Patient Support Officer.

Queensland Health advertisement for a cleaner

Cold sore event through window

Many of these events have an association with those time periods when a person's immune system is weakened or stressed. If compromised a person's immune system, which under normal circumstances is able to keep the herpes virus particles in check, is overwhelmed and a window of opportunity for cold sore formation is opened.

www.animated-teeth.com

Continuously improve! Continuously improve!

Incorporating a top-down and a bottom-up approach to planning, Strategic Directions for Health 1998-2003 represented a shared commitment to continuously improve and build on quality health care and service for the people of NSW.

NSW Health Department

Death by outcome

No one is denying that there have been some bad patient outcomes.

Leonie Raven, Queensland Department of Health, talking about the death and maiming of patients in Bundaberg Hospital, *The Age*, 9 July 2005

Deep administration and powerful commitment

Mr. Martin and Dr. Merlino will bring deep administrative and clinical experience and a powerful commitment to transforming Kings County's behavioral health services into a model program focused on recovery and rehabilitation, and designed around principles of compassion, patient empowerment, family engagement, and clinical best practices.

Press release from the New York City Health and Hospitals Corporation

Developing a tool

The Cochrane Consumers and Communication Review Group invites you to a seminar on: 'What do to do when the evidence tells you something you don't want to know? Developing a tool to assist with examining and translating evidence to practice and policy.'

A 'collaborative initiative' involving the Department of Human Services Victoria, Statewide Quality Branch

Enhanced NEF

Please note that HACC MDS V2 National Electronic Form (NEF) application will also be available free of charge in June. This will be enhancing the existing NEF to accommodate V2 reporting requirements and updating to more flexible underlying technology. This will satisfy the National HACC MDS V2 reporting requirements. Please note that various jurisdictions may have their own additional data reporting elements.

Email from HACC Outcomes Section, Australian Government Department of Health and Ageing

Hospital to brand patients?

Your brand is the visual identity that sets you apart from your competitors. It incorporates and communicates your core business, your market position and your values. Developing and maintaining the integrity of your brand across all communications is paramount.

Dzign Diezel Group, engaged by the board of Mount Alexander Hospital in Castlemaine, Victoria, to 'undertake a review of the the branding' of the hospital

Identified requirements

The HACC [Home and Community Care] MDS V2 User Guide, when used in conjunction with the technical specifications on the website, will identify the data transmission requirements. The HACC MDS V2 User Guide requires endorsement by HACC Officials in mid May. Once endorsed, all documentation will be updated to reflect the User Guide requirements on the website. This should provide developers with all the information they require to implement HACC MDS V2.

Email from HACC Outcomes Section, Department of Health and Ageing

Identify! Identify! Implement! Implement!

The forum will have relevance to divisions' new funding contracts and performance indicators, and for implementation of the National Chronic Disease Strategy.

From an email invitation from the Australian Divisions of General Practice, February 2005

Identifying impacts

In the continuation of this journey, the Conference

aim is to address the need to identify what has been the impact of getting research right?

From a flyer for the 2006 GP (General Practice) & PHC (Primary Health Care) Research Conference, entitled 'Optimising Impact'

Implemented gaps

Using process mapping and involving both clinical and administrative staff, gaps and areas for improvement were identified and then implemented.

Churchill Consultants

Improved infection control survey indicators

With regard to the cleaning regime I can assure you that the schedule for cleaning has not been downgraded since the acquisition of the hospital. In fact the hospital has invested in upgrading cleaning equipment and improved its infection control survey indicators by approximately 25% in the past 12 months.

Reply from the CEO of Calvary John James Hospital

A key strategic intent

Please see attached Memo about a standardisation program for the Western Pathology Cluster. I am sending this out to signal a key strategic intent and to initiate the process, but the outcomes will depend on the hard work that is to follow, the leadership of those who will drive the process and all those who engage in the journey.

Memo sent from the NSW Health Western Pathology cluster

Loyal patients

Patient Loyalty: Leaving patients with a positive feeling about the care they received is the primary goal, however the organization's viability rests on whether those feelings are translated into a tendency to use the facility for future healthcare needs – in other words, whether the organization is building loyal patients. Loyalty, more so than just satisfaction, is statistically linked to financial and growth metrics and overall sustainability. In addition to measuring patient loyalty soon after care, the system meets JCAHO requirements for pain management, education, and safety.

Gallup Consulting

Our commitment

We are committed to helping you and your partner achieve a positive birth experience.

Prince of Wales Private Hospital

Out of harm events' way

A four-year study at Sydney Children's Hospital found the program led to the number of harm events being cut by more than 50 per cent . . .

The Australian, 20 November 2008

Pragmatic corporate strategic intent – made simple

Our services

- Development of pragmatic corporate strategic intent and objectives that respond to environmental challenges and internal strengths and weaknesses

- Aligning an organisation's system and cultural dimensions to achieve the business strategy

Strategy is a frequently touted management term that is often misused and misinterpreted. At Churchill we believe that strategy is simply the determination of what should be done – given the current situation and where we want to be in the future.

Churchill Consultants

Rebalance focus, quantify impact, review paradigms and develop a roadmap – now!

To rebalance focus and improve systemic governance and management of the public health system asset base, there are changes needed at all levels of the system.

Enhance the role of Health Purchasing Victoria in the coordination of procurement and expanding preferred supplier arrangements with documented pricing points for identified periods and identified capital items.

Conduct forums for suppliers to present a range of appropriate financing options to Health Services for the procurement of Non-major capital items, and to answer questions about market dynamics and the future of the supplier market . . .

A comprehensive project should be undertaken in the next 12 months to address funding policy and structure, processes, practices, procurement options and business case development, addressing the following as preferred options:

- develop a road map to move from a program-based approach to an entity-based model, which aligns with the governance and accountability of Boards and senior management, and is based on Health Services asset replacement and strategic plans.

The Victorian Healthcare Association Ltd

Robust solutions

Healthcare organizations face many significant challenges today including acute financial pressures, increasing competition, human resource shortages, patient safety concerns, and growth in healthcare consumption. Overcoming these challenges requires innovative and robust solutions to achieve sustainable improvement and superior performance. Over the last 50 years, Gallup developed a series of healthcare-specific, research-based solutions to assist healthcare leaders in addressing this ever-changing environment. While each of these solutions provides improved performance, combining them into an integrated and aligned suite of initiatives provides exponential results.

Gallup Consulting

Shop till you drop

The Clinic at Walmart: A direct link between the community and local hospitals

Over the next two years, we intend to partner with local hospitals to open 'The Clinic at Walmart' co-branded clinics in our stores. These co-branded clinics will be directly linked to the hospitals our customers already know and trust.

www.walmartstores.com

Small footprint, high leverage

Churchill Consulting is a boutique consulting firm specialising in organisational performance and improvement.

Churchill was founded in 2002.

We are focussed on WA organisations seeking strategic counsel.

We work in partnership with clients.

We maintain a small footprint, high leverage approach

We ensure knowledge transfer with an emphasis on senior practitioners

We provide independence and value

Churchill Consulting

Sociocultural social constructs of health

Viewing health and physical activity as social constructs

Viewing health as a social construct involves viewing health from a sociocultural perspective(from the viewpoint of society as a whole). In this way we can look at the underlying causes or contributing factors relating to health status.

From *Personal Development, Health and Physical Education*, a text book

Unintended benefit leakage

Fraud in health industry speak is often called 'unintended benefit leakage' – a bland description for a rotten practice. Unintended benefit leakage, or fraud, occurs when claims are made for medical services not rendered.

Senator Cory Bernardi, *Hansard*, 18 October 2006

Unitary humans

A mentoring moment is an intersubjective coming to know in dialogue that engages unitary humans in a transformative process, confirming beliefs and values in creatively imagining and launching projects . . . The human-to-human engagement in a mentoring moment is unpredictable and everchanging as value priorities shift with different experiences and new understandings.

Nursing Science Quarterly, volume 15, issue 2, April 2002

Utilisations of time

Employees are reminded that the non-trivial usage of Service resources, for reasons other than conducting Service business, is strictly forbidden . . . Any work time remaining after you have completed your position's required tasks should be utilised to assist other Service staff in their roles or to engage in quality improvement exercises.

Hospital CEO

What?

Ongoing parallel qualitative work indicates that explicit consideration of personal values attached to potential outcomes challenges women's perceptions of the optimal decision and this may influence their resolve to achieve a vaginal birth.

University of Bristol

Learnings exercises

A fun performance-based activity to be implemented singly, in pairs or in teams. Use each of these words and phrases in sentences about something you enjoy:

glom

sunset (verb)

actionable trends

road map

enabilisers

expertise (verb)

defined timeliness

circle the drain

Use each of these words and phrases in sentences about something that disturbs or frightens you:

ladders off

credit-blemished

timebox

in-market synergies

insurmountable opportunities

pipeline effect

immersive experience

looming uptick

This time, write the sentences in terms of a favourite animal:

> *functionality suite*
> *defined timeliness*
> *FIFO basis*
> *iteration*
> *dewatered*
> *close that time box*
> *outleting*

Now write about a loved one:

> *dynamic rightsizing*
> *under-penetrated*
> *meat on the bone*
> *big fulcrum event*
> *target hardening*
> *backcasting*
> *vertical stovepipe*
> *dedicated recovery time*
> *low-hanging fruit*
> *robust high-availability solution*
> *legacy position*

Compare your sentences with the professional examples below. Using the examples as a perfect ten, estimate your scores.

> There's no doubt that this is the beginning of the recession and there's no sign that the end is near and certainly no sign of any looming *uptick*.
>
> Shane Oliver, AMP Capital Investors

> In the morning, I wake up, I have a special Google alert to the Baltic dry shipping index, because I'm trying to *glom* into something positive.
>
> Larry Kudlow, CNBC, March 2009

Bluestring, Xdrive and AOL Pictures will be *sunset*.
[They] haven't gained sufficient traction in the
marketplace or the monetization levels necessary.

Kevin Conroy, executive vice president of AOL, 14 July 2008

If they can't get their heads together, there's no way
we're going to get *meat on the bone*.

Talking head, CNBC, March 2009

Accredited Home Lenders Holding Co. became the
latest player in mortgages to the poor and *credit-blemished*
to admit that it was grappling with a liquidity shortfall.

The Times, 14 March 2007

Citi's audio brand was composed especially for Citi
and *ladders off* our purpose of 'Driving Success'.

Citibank

But it was the head of another Swiss bank, Peter Wuffli,
then the president of UBS, who set the standard for
obfuscation in February 2003 when he referred to
the major cutbacks occasioned by the dotcom crash as
'*dynamic rightsizing*'.

www.ft.com

SOL TRUJILLO: In terms of where we focus our efforts in
relation to solutions consistent with my presentation,
the good news in terms of opportunity is that we are
still quite *under-penetrated* in data take-up, so it is very low
single digits in terms of data attach rates, and even the
adoption of smart phones is really at the beginning of
an adoption curve.

Telstra Investor Day, November 2008

Synergy helps Honda implement a *robust high-availability solution* to reduce the risk of system downtime, plus increase server capacity to accommodate growth in the business.

www.synergy.com.au

Hence a key threshold activity of the project was to determine what *functionality suite* would be appropriate to the needs of Victoria and could also be financially justified.

Phil Perry, Principal of Impaq Consulting writing about the rollout in Victoria of 'advanced' electricity meters in the June edition of Metering International

Sometimes trends can hide pretty well, and one of Google Analytics' jobs is to make the most *actionable trends* as apparent as possible so you can surface them to your colleagues and management (and get a promotion). And we realize that most management reporting is done in weekly and monthly time buckets.

www.weaselwords.com.au

Let's just close that *time box* and move on to the next topic.

www.weaselwords.com.au

We appreciate Dell showing strong support for the bulk of our product offering and the strength of our *road map*.

Scott McLaughlin, a spokesman for California-based Intel

Preferred initiatives will display the following design: . . . *Defined timeliness*, or 'ripeness' of conditions in the operating landscape of the project.

Application guideline from the ANZ Trustees Program: National Charitable Initiative

We are looking at fuel economy *enabilisers*.

Head of Australian car manufacturing company

Once the teams are fully implemented and the projects are transitioned, each team will be processing information and projects *on a FIFO basis* (First-In, First-Out). That is, once a project is started, it will be completed up to its end point in the process before another is started.

From a memo to Products Specialists Regional Directors re: Project Management

It's a danger but in the sense the debt, I think, is a short deterrent because very few companies would take on that sort of gearing on day one, particularly since this deal is based on what we call *in-market Australian synergies*.

Trevor O'Hoy, Fosters CEO, on the merits of Fosters takeover of Southcorp, ABC radio

Hunter was a key contributor and mentor in the development of The Natural Advantage of Nations and has expressed genuine excitement at the *insurmountable opportunities* available to these groups, identifying Australia as having 'the potential to be a sustainability superpower'.

Natural Edge Project, Sustainable Business Practice Tour

Dt. Maurice Holmes of the Thomasville Police Department said, 'We're trying to educate the public on what we call *target hardening* which basically means making your property a little more secure.'

www.wctv.tv

The paper shows how a combination of forecasting and backcasting is necessary for predicting a water service provision model of the future. Using some real examples, we demonstrate how actions that pick the *low hanging fruit* result from forecasting and how actions that challenge existing assumptions result from *backcasting* . . .

www.weaselwords.com.au

We are saying you can give yourself a *dedicated recovery time* objective at a shared price point.

www.australianit.news.com.au

But the problem with that planning is that it had been done in the *vertical stovepipe* of that agency and the *horizontal connection* of those plans did not occur.

General Jay Garner to the British Government Future of Iraq Commission

A council representative is on scene and we've called for a structural engineer *to expertise* as to what may happen to this building.

Superintendent Craig Brierley, from the Fire Brigade,on cracks in a building next to the construction site for the new Surry Hills Community Centre. ABC News

Yes, my colleague is an expert in sustainable cities. He's putting together some notes for you. He's very good at *outleting*.

Overheard in a lift in the Victorian Department of Sustainability and Environment

Therefore, based on that *pipeline effect*, the $50 million provided under the new ANTA agreement in 2001, if they were entirely devoted to New Apprenticeships— bearing in mind that it is only 22 per cent of the system—would produce a pipeline requirement for funds in the out years of $50 million in 2001, $40 million in 2002, $31 million in 2003 and $22 million in 2004. Would you agree with that?

Senator Kim Carr

'We absolutely believe' there must be a '*second iteration* of a stimulus response . . .'

Canadian New Democratic Party leader Jack Layton, *Bloomberg*, March 2009

In London, New York, Paris, Milan, Barcelona and Melbourne, the same pattern is beginning to reveal itself: shopping is emerging as art, as cultural exchange, as *immersive experience*, as a way of learning.

The Future Laboratory Melbourne Retail Strategy

Sometimes, when *big fulcrum events* occur, days like June 30 a few weeks ago, and nothing of consequence happens, you have to step back and ask, 'What the heck is wrong with this market?'

'What's Really Wrong with the Market', Jim Cramer, 13 June 2004

Virtually all the losses were from *legacy positions* that had already been there.

John Thain, CEO Merill Lynch

In Washington, politicians are making hay with the public's perception that greedy CEOs and executives were asleep at the switch as their companies *circled the drain*.

www.corporate-eye.com/

Conclusion

'Without distinction of speech there is never much distinction of idea.' In a forgotten book called *Dialectic* by a forgotten author called Frank Binder, that observation was made before people spoke of *learnings*, before they got wet in *weather events* and wondered if *fire activity* would *impact upon* them, and when *team-building* was recommended in the main by scoutmasters and totalitarians.

In 1932 Mr Binder could not know that in attempting to make a case for lively and articulate expression, he had gone as close as anyone has to stating the primary aim of modern management language. (That's the dialectic for you.) After all, it is easy to imagine a spin doctor whispering in the ear of a politician or CEO before a press conference: 'Remember, without distinction of speech there is never much distinction of idea.' As if anyone half media-savvy doesn't know to give them no more than what he wants to give them. If he wants to give them nothing he'll give them that. If he must give them more than nothing, he won't give them anything concrete. Give them abstractions, clichés, the same instant platitudes over and over. Give them muck.

It is just as easy to picture the author of a consultant's report finding comfort in Binder's dictum upon realising that she hasn't a clue what she is trying to say, or if indeed there is anything to be said at all; or a teacher labouring over a school report; or a student struggling with an essay. For those who do not have an idea or do not understand what it is they are meant to have ideas about, management language is specifically indicated: not to provide the user with ideas, but to mask the absence of them – more than mask it, *guarantee* it.

Because there is this advantage to management language as well: wherever it is spoken, no livelier language can find a footing; and, as a consequence, no ideas can either. The stuff is noxious and systemic. As certain plants adapt to an environment and eventually dominate it, management language has adapted to the needs of power in the environment of modern organisations. Less a language than a means of organising and regimenting behaviour – or *behaviours*, as it would have us say, for no apparent reason – management speak evolved in the relative confinement of large companies but, finding favourable elements outside, spread like gorse and blackberries into every field of public life. As those weeds smother all the varieties of indigenous life, management language smothers both vernacular and formal English with the same efficiency and obliterates the signs of its existence.

The language of management has thus become the language not only of company managers and their staff, but of civil servants of all kinds, including university administrators, teachers, librarians, police, firefighters and local government officials. It has invaded sport and even religion. And because it is abstract, pompous and obscure, this language is as if made for contemporary culture's crucial meeting of media and politics. With what else could we fill the present moment: the infinite succession of them, unfolding – always *unfolding* – into stories on the 24/7 news cycle? With what else could we stuff our consciousness, at this point in time, going forward?

May the Lord be with us all as we move forward.

Cardinal George Pell, Advent letter

*I acknowledge with thanks my debt to all those people who send me
(and the Weasel Words website) fragments of the language of their working lives.
For research and all-round collaboration and assistance, I am grateful to
Helen Smith. My thanks also to Meredith Curnow at Random House for
unfailing support; to Julian Welch for able and assiduous editing; and to the
inimitable Bruce Petty, for obvious reasons.*